THE
SAINT FRANCIS
MURALS
OF
SANTA FE

THE COMMISSION AND THE ARTISTS

THE
SAINT FRANCIS
MURALS
OF
SANTA FE

THE COMMISSION AND THE ARTISTS

Carl Sheppard

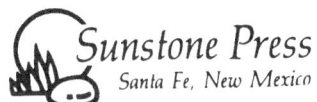

Sunstone Press
Santa Fe, New Mexico

Library of Congress Cataloging in Publication Data:

Sheppard, Carl D., 1916-
    The Saint Francis murals of Santa Fe : the commission and the artists / Carl Sheppard.
       p.   cm.
    Includes bibliographical references.
       ISBN: 0-86534-137-0   : $9.95
    1. Mural painting and decoration, American — New Mexico — Santa Fe. 2. Mural painting and decora-
tion — 20th century — New Mexico — Santa Fe. 3. Francis, of Assisi, Saint, 1182-1226 — Art. 4. Clare, of
Assisi, Saint 1194-1253 — Art. 5. Columbus, Christopher — Portraits. 6. Mayas — Pictorial works.
7. Beauregard, Donald — Criticism and interpretation. 8. Chapman, Kenneth M. — Criticism and interpretation. 9. Vierra, Carlos — Criticism and interpretation. 10. Saint Francis Auditorium (Museum of Fine Arts
(Museum of New Mexico)) 11. Santa Fe (N.M.) — Buildings, structures, etc. I. Title.
ND2638.S27S54   1989
751.7'3'0978956--dc20   89-39446
                                                                                                   CIP

Published in 1989 by SUNSTONE PRESS
             Post Office Box 2321
             Santa Fe, NM 87504-2321 / USA

Dedicated to

Christine, Nancy and Katharine

and Cousin Erma

CONTENTS

ILLUSTRATIONS

THE MURALS

A. "Apotheosis of St. Francis," St. Francis Auditorium, Santa Fe, NM, oil on canvas, 5'6" wide as are all the center panels of the triptychs, including the gilt frame around the panels; the side panels of the triptychs are 3'5" wide and include only one side frame strip. All photographs of the murals are courtesy of the Museum of New Mexico, Museum of Fine Arts.

B. "Vision of Columbus at La Rábida," St. Francis Auditorium, Santa Fe, NM.

C. "Preaching to the Mayas and the Aztecs," St. Francis Auditorium, Santa Fe, NM.

D. "Building of the Missions in New Mexico," St. Francis Auditorium, Santa Fe, NM.

E. "Conversion of St. Francis," St. Francis Auditorium, Santa Fe, NM.

F. "Renunciation of Santa Clara," St. Francis Auditorium, Santa Fe, NM.

G. "Conversion of St. Francis," Donald Beauregard, watercolor and pencil on paper, 18" x 10 1/2" Courtesy Museum of New Mexico, Photographic Archive, No. 13987, Museum of New Mexico artifact No. 1146/23P.

H. "Vision of Columbus at La Rábida," Donald Beauregard, watercolor and pencil on paper, 16" x 18" courtesy Museum of New Mexico, Photographic Archive, No. 38305, Museum of New Mexico artifact No. 1150/23P.

PREFACE

Many pleasant concerts and stimulating lectures gave me ample opportunity to gaze at the interior of the Saint Francis Auditorium of the Museum of Fine Arts, part of the Museum of New Mexico, in Santa Fe. The decorative murals attract special attention, at first for a rapid survey and then for a growing focus. Predominantly blue and green highlighted by reds and yellows, the murals clothe the white walls of the auditorium without intrusion, attractively, and with distinction.

I began to wonder why these pictures are there. I looked for a program but was frustrated by what I found which seemed to have only scant reference to Saint Francis and none to Santa Fe. A placard states brief information about the cycle of paintings but is strangely vague as to the meaning of the murals and as to the artists who accomplished the project.

So I decided to uncover the mystery that surrounds the paintings and found to my surprise the tragedy of Donald Beauregard and clarified his contributions to the murals and those of Kenneth Chapman and Carlos Vierra.

For encouragement and assistance on this project I would like to thank: Patricia Sheppard, Orlando Romero, Richard Rudisill, Arthur Olivas, Sandra D'Emilio, James Romero, and Phyllis Cohen.

All letters quoted in the text may be found in the History Library of the Museum of New Mexico. The quotation of Saint Francis concerning his conversion is from "Saint Francis of Assisi" by Johannes Jorgensen, based on "The Little Flowers of Saint Francis".

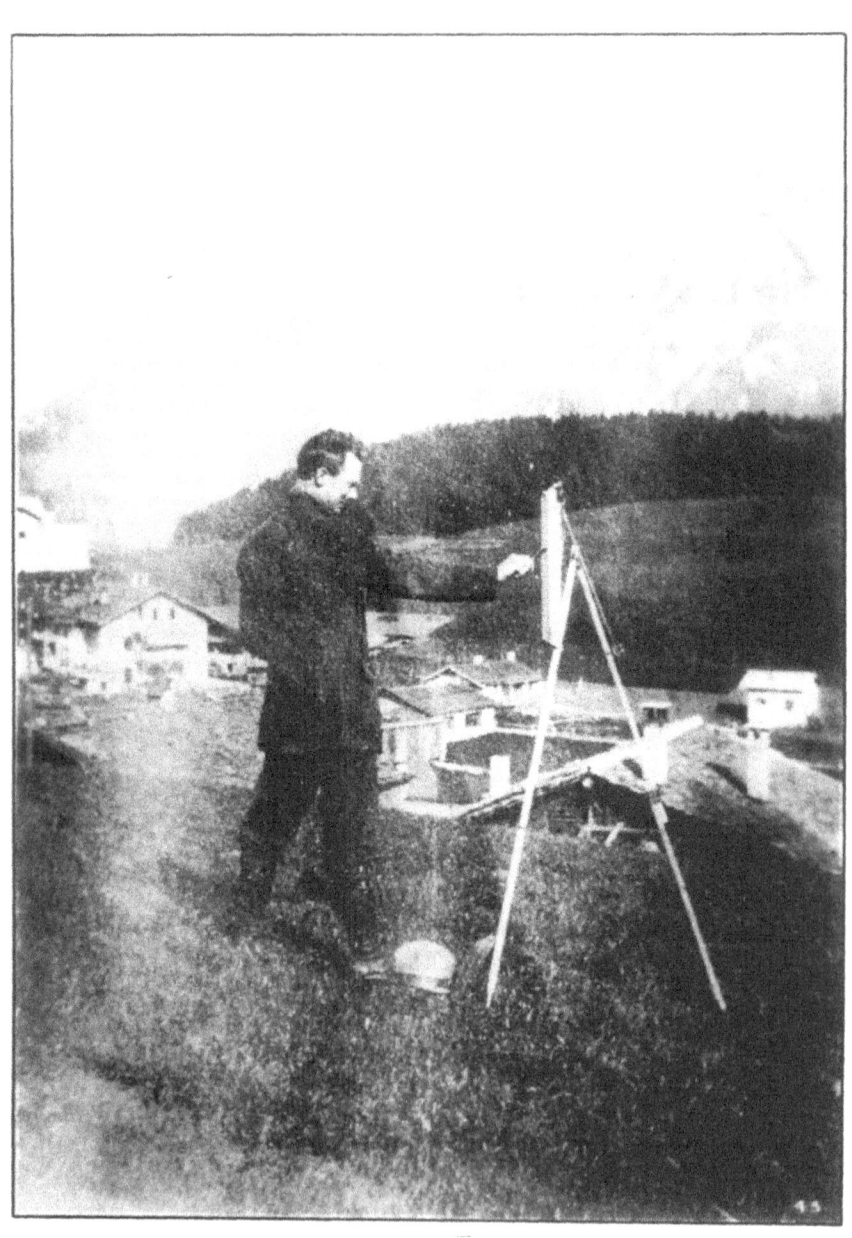

Daniel Beauregard, painting in Switzerland, 1913.

CHAPTER I

THE MURALS

The Saint Francis Auditorium in the Museum of Fine Arts of the Museum of New Mexico encloses the most imposing and romantic public space in the City of Santa Fe, New Mexico. It is a handsome, ample room, with a rear balcony and a choir-like projection so that one is inevitably reminded of Hispanic church architecture of the seventeenth century in the area of the Rio Grande, even to the use of a transverse clerestory across the nave in front of the choir. The prototype of the auditorium is indeed a mission church, such as that at Acoma, at Pecos or at Ranchos de Taos in New Mexico.

The entry into the auditorium from the street is through two massive wooden doors set within a recess formed by flanking two-story towers. A balcony breaks the recess at the second floor and suggests access to the interior balcony through a door. Inside, the balcony makes a relatively low entrance room through which a visitor moves to the exhilarating height of the main hall. The floor is covered with stone slabs of deep grey tones; the walls are rough finished plaster to resemble hand-finished whitewashed adobe; the ceilings are supported on huge, roughly hewn wooden beams (vigas) supported on double corbels, all darkened as if by smoke. Across the vigas rest aspen stakes set diagonally. The whole repertory of the visible construction materials and of the materials of the decorative detailing are traditional to the Rio Grande even to the brightly colored chisel gouges along the lower edges of both the vigas and corbels.

The interior is massive, weighty in effect, shadowed because of the few windows in the sides of the hall, glowing at the end from the light entering through the unseen clerestory *(Figure 1 and Figure 6)* The quiet obscurity of the interior is evocative of the past: of Pueblo Indians, of dusty trails for conquest and conversion, of unpacified tribes, of flags, of kings and empire, of Moors, and of Mexicans who helped control the region for the Spanish Crown and then for themselves, and finally of the "gringos" who conquered the territory and defended it against forces from the South during the Civil War.

All the above is involved metaphorically in the auditorium of Saint Francis. In addition was the belief that the Native Americans of the New Mexico region had been occupying the landscape for not just a millenium and a half but for many millenia. Where did they come from? Were they the Lost Tribes of Israel? Were their petroglyphs of a Phoenician origin? Did the Aztecs influence the development of the people now settled there? Did their roots reach Central America and the benign civilization of the Maya? The patron of the auditorium thought so!

At the rear of the hall and above the present platform, suitable for performances, is a slightly inset niche topped by a segmental curve. Within this recess is placed, as originally planned, an oil mural framed so as to make a triptych, the two side wings being equal to the middle scene. The subject is identified as the "Apotheosis of Saint Francis *(Color Section A)*. To the right in the eastern arm of the the choir is another oil painting; this one is identified as "The Vision of Columbus at La Rábida" *(Color Section B)*. Along the east wall of the hall is a second triptych: "Preaching to the Mayas and the Aztecs" *(Color Section C)*. A little further is a single panel of "Building

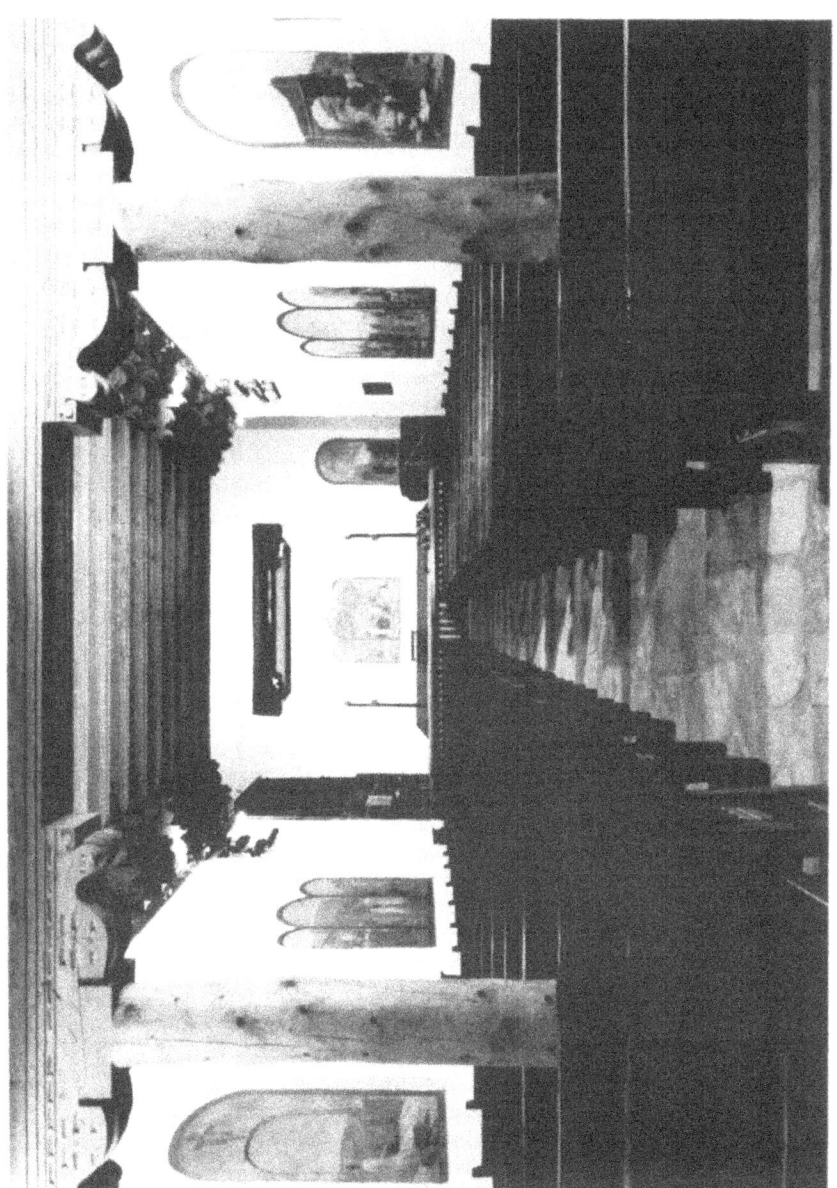

Figure 1: *Saint Francis Auditorium, Santa Fe, NM., interior from the south, March, 1988.*

the Missions in New Mexico" *(Color Section D).* On the wall opposite is another panel: "The Conversion of Saint Francis" *(Color Section E).* or variously "Saint Francis Renounces His Worldly Goods," as does Saint Clare in the accompanying third triptych *(Color Section F).*

The subjects of these murals show a fascinating and unique iconography or series of subjects, only three of which deal directly or indirectly with Saint Francis himself: "The Conversion," the Saint Clare painting and the "Apotheosis," and, except for the first, do not deal with the episodes of humility and poverty and love of man and nature usually associated with the founder of the Franciscan Order. Except for the "Conversion," the Santa Fe scenes do not occur in the famous 14th century cycle of frescoes Giotto painted in the upper church of San Francesco at Assisi in Umbria and which came to be accepted as the standard Franciscan themes. Why the emphasis in New Mexico on sublimation of the Saint? Why emphasize Saint Clare? What has Columbus to do with Saint Francis or, for that matter, the Maya and the construction of buildings in the New World?

As frequently happens to monuments of antiquity, their meanings become obscured and lost. This is certainly the case with the murals of the auditorium, although the patron of the building certainly knew what he meant to provide by his commission for the hall. The key to the murals' significance must be sought through the writings and actions of the patron, i.e., in the thoughts of Edgar Lee Hewett, Director of the School of American Archeology of the American Institute of Archeology, Director of the Museum of New Mexico (both of Santa Fe) as well as Director of Exhibits for the Panama-California Exposition at San Diego, California. He was an extraordinary intellectual entrepreneur. The financial patron and politician was Frank Springer, a lawyer made wealthy through the litigation concerning the great Maxwell Land Grant in northern New Mexico. There were others who contributed a great deal, particularly political clout with the Legislature of New Mexico at Santa Fe, but Hewett and Springer were dominant and it was Edgar Lee Hewett who pioneered the philosophical and moral directions of the institutions he founded and administered. It didn't matter so much who originated an idea; it was Hewett, within the purview of the institutions, who decided on its merits and Springer who usually paid the bill or funded the deficit.

Santa Fe, although the capital of the Territory, was a small provincial town in 1910 of only 5,071 inhabitants of mixed heritage: Hispanic, Native American, and Anglo. Hewett exploited both local potential and national attention and interest far beyond anything imagined by Santa Feans, thereby earning their questioning gratitude. The Villa Real de la Santa Fe was fortunate to have attracted a man with as much qualification as he had garnered.

In addition to their unique symbolism, the murals of the auditorium hold a tragedy and further mystery. The artist commissioned to create the series, Donald Beauregard, died as a young man before he completed much more than sketches for the project. Hewett had to find other artists to complete the program. Letters from him indicated that with the approval of Springer he selected Carlos Vierra and Kenneth Chapman to do the job. The murals themselves, however, hold the secrets of how much should be credited to Beauregard and how much of the completed work was accomplished by Chapman and Vierra and which of them did what.

Starting on the left, the mural panels are arranged in a chronological sequence, however intermittent it may seem. "The Conversion of Saint Francis" is first and as a subject dates from the thirteenth century. Kneeling on the side of an arched entrance in a stone wall the young Francis gazes, with head tilted back, over a single burning candle placed in a holder on an altar-like block and across the open space of the entrance way. Slightly to one side of the keystone of the arch above floats a crucifixion, shaped like a devotional 13th century Tuscan painting of the subject. A burst of light glows against the cross from behind, silhouetting the object. Through the open portal, a precipitous drop carries down a presumed staircase or trail over to a few distant cypresses and a white wall curving up a blue-green hillside to fortified Assisi, crouched on its hilltop, profiled against a lighter blue sky.

The young man holds out his empty hands, palms up. He is dressed only in a white thigh-length tunic with short sleeves; his other garments are spread out in an undifferentiated mass in front of him. With its panoramic view of the Umbrian country-side, with the solitariness of the figure stretching out its arms in a gesture of longing or submission, the mural indicates a personal mystery — an enlightenment, perhaps an understanding? There is not much to help us interpret the scene except the darkening landscape, the single lit candle and the floating image of the crucified Christ, Christian and mystic symbols of possible transfiguration. Certainly the emphasis is personal and individual. What a contrast of interpretation to that of Giotto's fresco of "Saint Francis Renounces His Worldly Goods" *(Figure 2).*

At Assisi, the young man stands in a public square, surrounded by people; a bishop quickly wraps a cloth around his body,

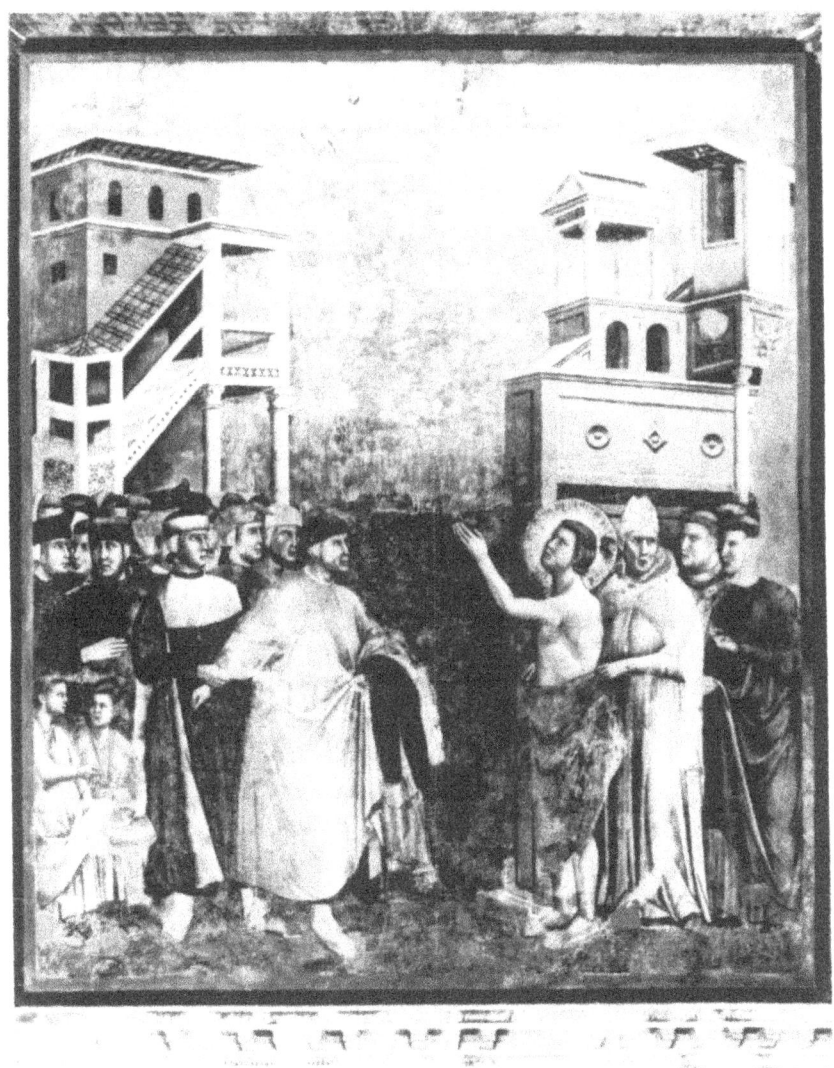

Figure 2: *"Saint Francis Renounces His Worldly Goods,"* Giotto di Bondone, fresco, Upper Church, San Francesco, Assisi.

naked since he has just cast off his luxurious garments. St. Francis has renounced his inheritance before his father who has brought him to the ecclesiastic court to disinherit him. This is a public event, witnessed by many people. The action has public import and carries the shock of unconventionality. At the auditorium in Santa Fe the conversion is private, exclusive, totally personal. It is an event revealed to an audience to whom the emotional reality of religion is extremely personal and tolerant of many variations and interpretations.

Actually the Santa Fe scene is a conflation of the "Conversion" and the "Renunciation" according to tradition. In the chapel of San Damiano, a small field church in ruins, Saint Francis frequently prayed for guidance. "Great and glorious God, my Lord Jesus Christ! I implore thee to enlighten me and to disperse the darkness of my soul! Give me true faith and firm hope and a perfect charity! Grant me, O Lord, to know thee so well that in all things I may act by the light and in accordance with thy holy will!" From the crucifix came a voice: "Now go hence, Francis, and build up my house for it is nearly falling down."

By contrast, the "Renunciation of Santa Clara," as the identification of the triptych reads, is a procession or gathering of people both mundane and spiritual, with an act of kindness by Saint Francis added to it *(Figure 3 and Color Section F)*. The panels exist separately so far as subject is concerned but the background offers a single scene from the shallow foreground all the way to the blue hills behind. In the middle panel, Saint Clare is poised gracefully taking a short step forward, her arms stretched out low at her sides. Her white skin is heightened by the white shift she wears; her other clothes are heaped at her

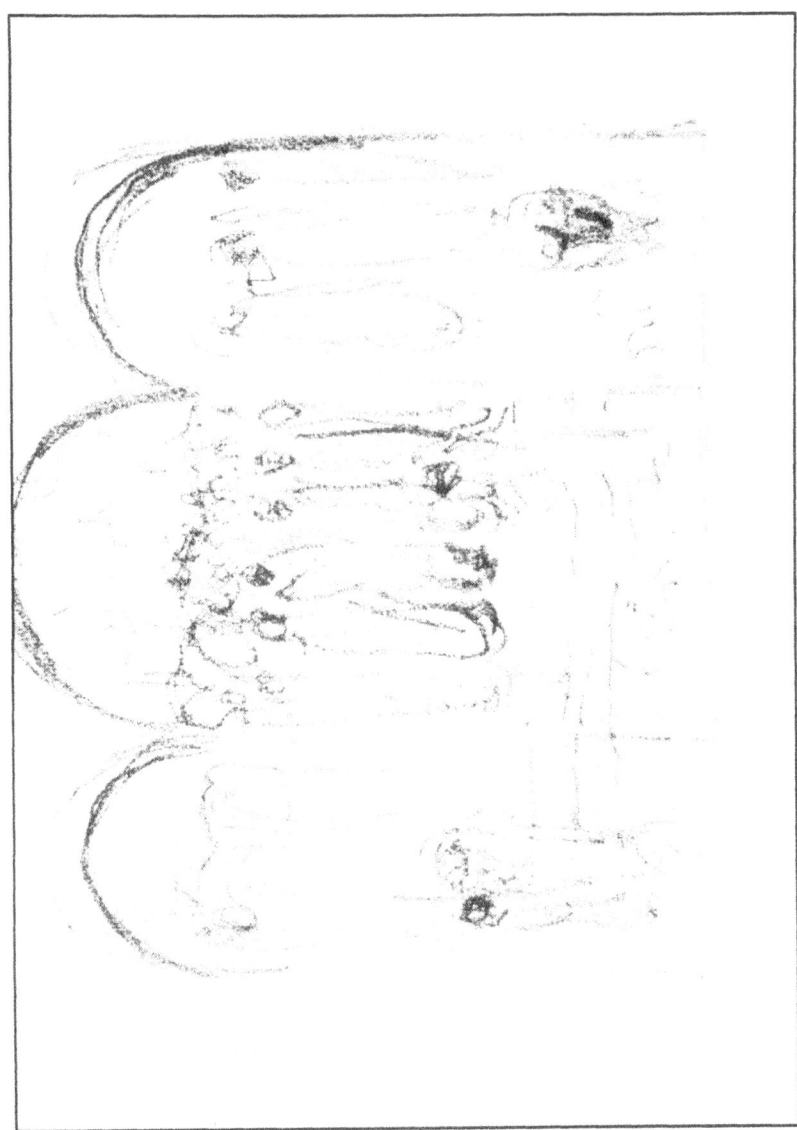

Figure 3: *Sketch for the "Renunciation of Santa Clara," Donald Beauregard.*

feet. She is petite, almost adolescent and apparently somnolent. Held out to her is a single white rose as is also a single red rose. These are offered by slender, graceful, floating female forms, whose bodies are barely visible through their transparent draperies, some of which rise in the air above them. A third female presence wafts towards the group with another flower from the right panel. These spirits, or angels, or virtuous embodiments, receive Clare pleasantly. Opposite them at the extreme left of the middle panel and supported by the frame is another female figure, seemingly in despair at Clare's action. Is she Clare's mother, or a personification of material well-being, for example?

The panel on the left is peopled as if it represented a halt by Chaucer's Pilgrims on their way to Canterbury. These are different types, male and female, who are not overwhelmed by Saint Clare's quiet renunciation. At least no glance directly looks upon it, although each individual seems somewhat disturbed by the situation, with the exception of the good-looking young man on horseback. In the three panels, only the woman veiled in white reacts strongly either positively or negatively. The scene is presented as a demonstration of piety, of purity, of grace, of female humility in a peaceful, beautiful world.

In the foreground of the right panel, Saint Francis appears. He cleanses the bloodied hand of a peasant whose crutch lies on the path next to them. The crutch suggests the peasant is ill or suffers from some bodily distress. There are many incidents recorded between Saint Francis and lepers; this may be one. Most people have referred to the man as a thief. Although Saint Francis certainly succored many persons, his gentle devotion to life itself has usually been symbolized by the theme of birds flocking fearlessly to him.

In the place of honor in the hall has been placed the "Apotheosis of St. Francis," *(Color Section A)*, a triptych rather comparable in its clear emptiness to the Saint Clare composition. Seven people occupy the foreground of the "Apotheosis." The landscape behind them stretches its empty greensward to the horizon through trees in foliage; the color scheme is again predominantly blue and green. Saint Francis kneels by a cascading spring and offers a golden chalice to a woman dressed in a flowing white garment. Behind her, half hidden by a bush, is another woman dressed in contrasting dark clothes with a hood over her head. On the left, slightly back, is a woman in a loose reddish garment. She looks pensively through the distant trees. In her left hand is an artist's palette and several brushes. She must be a personification. Perhaps the others, except Saint Francis, are likewise.

To the left of Saint Francis stands a young man barely clothed in a white sheet-like wrapping. Clutching his right hand to his chest, he gazes outward and upward, unaware of the golden cup proffered by Saint Francis. In the right-hand panel, an old man, at least his hair is white, is seated, head in profile, resting his chin on his lifted right hand. His upper body is bare, a dark cloak has slipped to the ground. Behind him a young woman lifts a baby to fruit hanging in a tree.

The landscape and the people inhabiting it are not engaged together in a single activity; each seems more isolated than communicative. Each is reserved in action and posture. The garden, beautiful as it is, is empty of all negative suggestion. Are these people in the Elysian Fields or perhaps on Parnassus? If so, why is the saint offering his chalice? The scene is ambiguous. Who termed it "Apotheosis"? It is not apparent that it is one even if Saint Francis kneels in the center of it.

Of great help in deciphering the meaning of the mural is a sketch *(Figure 4)* prepared for it with the identifying words beneath each of the characters except the Saint: from left to right they are ART, THEOLOGY, RELIGION, LITERATURE, PHILOSOPHY, and SOCIETY. It is certainly very strange to have Saint Francis offer a chalice to Religion with Theology lurking in the shadows behind. Saint Francis does not even show the signs of his stigmata. These were not shown either in the panel in which the Saint assists the peasant, yet they are usually heralded as the greatest mystery of the Saint. The personifications seem oddly chosen likewise. Perhaps experience was related to Religion and legality to Theology. It is individual exaltation through the humble offices of Saint Francis we are dealing with. We are not involved historically with Saint Frances nor with a traditional group of personifications. Perhaps the image suggests that those characteristics of Saint Francis by which he is revered—humility, love of all living things, poverty—are what he is offering to a world in which the creative and theological arts bring man intuitively into beauty as God created it.

The "Vision of Columbus at La Rábida" may have occurred at one of several visits. In 1488 Columbus and his son, Diego, arrived at the Monastery of La Rábida, Palos, Spain. Columbus had quit the Portuguese Court in despair of their help and was on his way to the Spanish Court at Cordova. He left Diego in care of the monks at the Monastery. In 1492 he returned from great disappointment at the Spanish Court to get Diego and

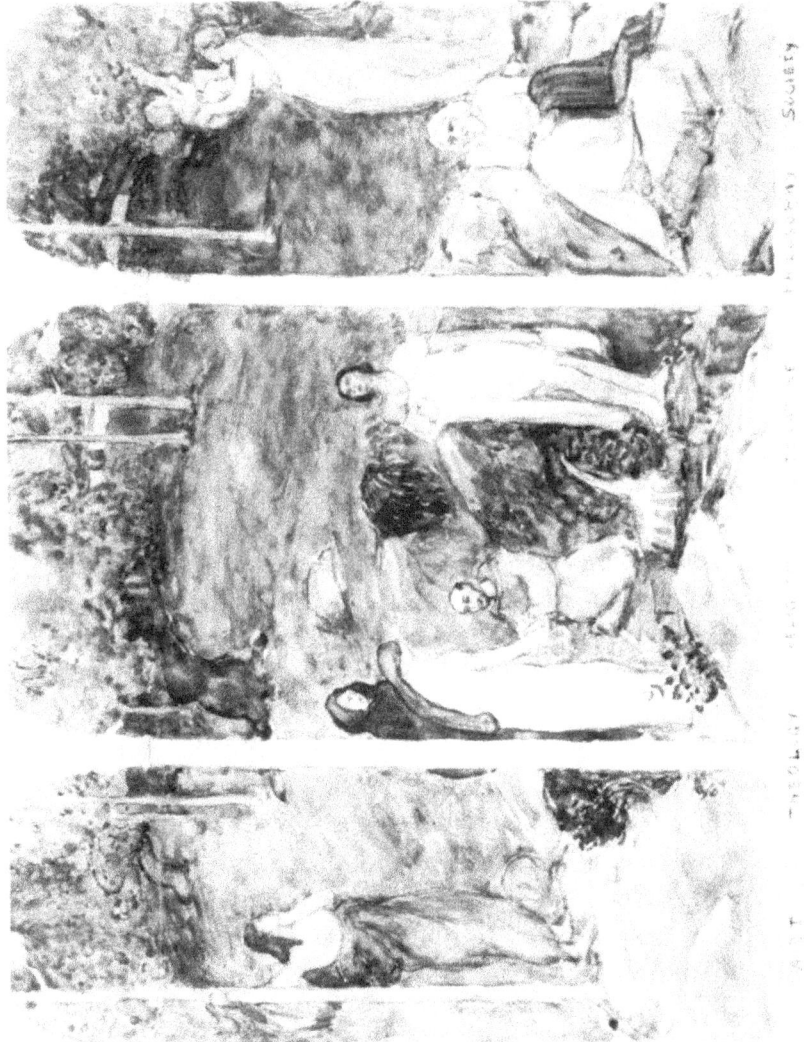

Figure 4: *Sketch for the "Apotheosis of St. Francis," Donald Beauregard.*

proceed to France. The head of the Monastery, Brother Juan Perez, had been confessor to Queen Isabella and had become a dedicated supporter of Columbus. They both returned to the Court at the camp of Santa Fe where the sovereigns were laying siege to Granada. Eventually, of course, Columbus was successful in his requests.

The artist treated the scene at La Rábida straightforwardly; Columbus and his son receive the hospitality of the Franciscan Monastery. A friar greets the two travelers. He motions welcome with his right hand and with his left presents a loaf of bread to the boy. The ships under full sail in the sky belong to Columbus who frowns in concentration as he looks at the cross embedded in the wall above the doorway. The visual report is direct enough but there are intimations of strong religious symbolism. The giving of bread following the offering of the cup by Saint Francis is no happenstance and refers to the divine presence of Christ— present in the "Apotheosis" as well as the "Vision". Apotheosis means exaltation or "making one with the gods." There appears here a mixture of classical and medieval philosophies. Transcendentalism is expressed metaphorically through the titles, personifications and actions of the murals.

That may be easy enough to understand, but what is Saint Francis doing with the chalice? The cup is possibly filled with water from the spring, the spring of life. It is not suggested in the mural that wine is in the cup. The symbolism does not carry that far nor that restrictively. Nevertheless, the wine and the bread of transubstantiation are intimated but yet left general enough to be accepted by almost any religious interpretation. After all, Catholics, Protestants, Mormons and Jews were all involved in the creation and execution of the murals. Transcendentalism underlies the entire mural cycle, a belief in a higher order to which man may attain.

The triptych of "Preaching to the Mayas and Aztecs," *(Color Section C)* balances the "Renunciation". The hypothetical event had to take place after 1542, the beginning of the conquest of Yucatan, and follows in chronological sequence after the "Vision of Columbus".

The left panel is filled with armed Spaniards and their horses and lances. The right panel has a Mayan background of temples from Palenque and Chichen Itza. Mayans in full regalia confront a Franciscan brother. He bows his head and holds aloft the figure of Christ on the cross as if the symbol were adequate to the mystery of conversion. No such peaceable meeting ever took place. The Maya were still revolting in 1697. The scene, however, accords with the peaceful ideal of a religious society in the context of the mural cycle.

The final mural is the most specific and balances the "Conversion" on the opposite wall — "Building of the Missions in New Mexico" *(Color Section D)*. Three friars are involved: one leans on a shovel, another holds a mallet and chisel and the third crouches over a plan with a compass in his hand. The three are probably not to be construed as actually taking part in construction but rather playing the role of instructor. Through a partially finished portal groups of Native Americans move up along a path to the heights of a rock mesa, which are hidden behind the portal.

The six scenes just examined can be understood as a projection of the moral ideals, the faiths and the interpretations of history as well as the aesthetic preferences of the dominant elite of Santa Fe at the time they were executed and put in place. The very name of the town, Santa Fe or Holy Faith, is the theme common to all the murals as each also concerns Saint Francis or his Order.

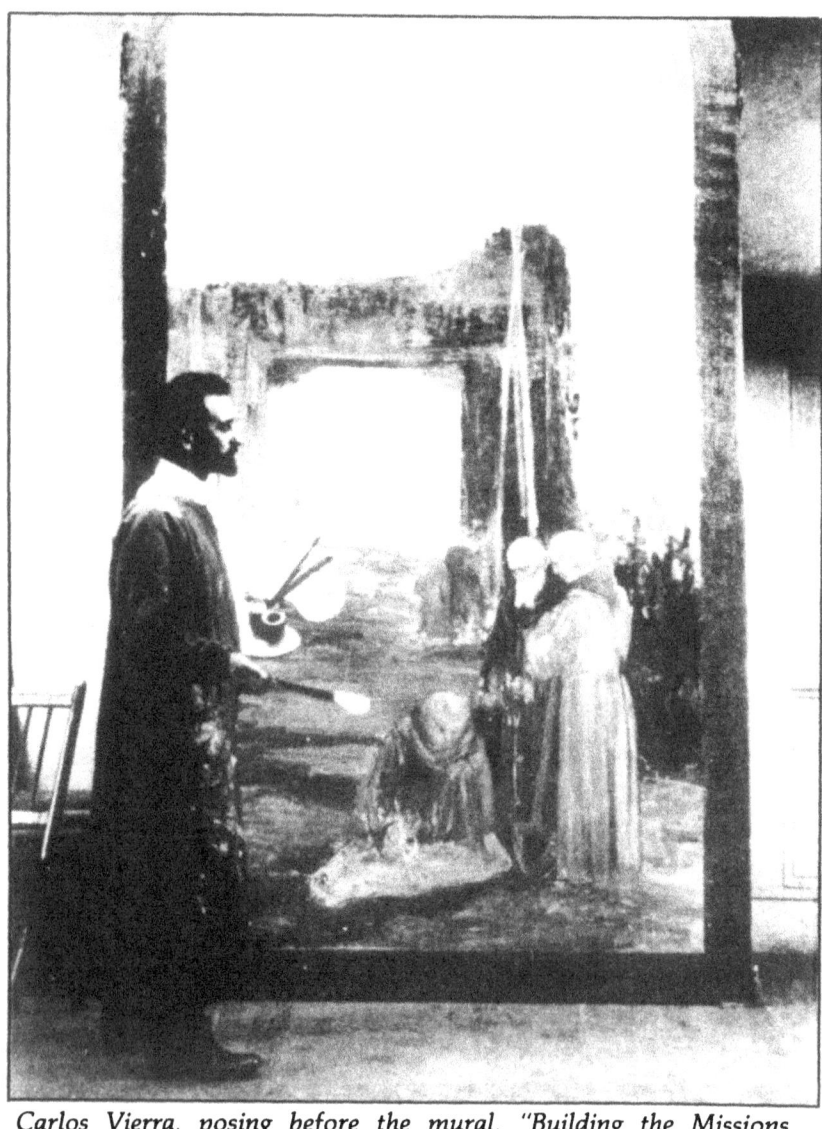

Carlos Vierra, posing before the mural, "Building the Missions of New Mexico," 1914.

CHAPTER II

THE COMMISSION

Dr. Hewett planned to use the Saint Francis murals first in the New Mexican pavilion at the Panama-California Exposition in San Diego. Financing for the New Mexico building and its exhibits along with many other commissions was easily available to Hewett as Director of Exhibits at San Diego. He made good use of his authority to the benefit of Santa Fe. Not only did he plan to use the murals again at Santa Fe, he also used the architect selected for the New Mexico building and had the structure later designed again for Santa Fe. Both are still standing — in San Diego the facade is recognizable, in Santa Fe the building is the Museum of Fine Arts, including the great auditorium.

Originally Hewett thought of a commission to be used in the New Mexico pavilion and then brought back to be displayed in the Palace of the Governors, just refurbished, actually redesigned with a Santa Fe portal as facade, by Sylvanus Morley and Jesse Nusbaum, working under the Director. As the San Diego Exposition matured so did Hewett's and Springer's ideas about the painting cycle. Possibly some of the anomalies in the cycle were caused by the fact that they were destined for San Diego instead of Santa Fe and also by the shift of the final use of the paintings from the Palace to the Museum of Fine Arts. It is not clear when a conclusion was reached as to the number let alone the specific subjects of the murals. In correspondence from Donald Beauregard, in Europe ostensibly to search out information about Saint Francis, there is a constant appeal for specific information on what the authorities at Santa Fe projected. He got no satisfactory answer, only that the cycle had to do with Saint Francis. Hewett had plenty of time to ruminate about the matter. Beauregard was in Europe in 1911 and returned in 1913 with only partial results so far as the murals were concerned. As to number, there are six murals now installed in the auditorium. Sketches for all six by Beauregard exist.

Photographs of the construction of the hall taken in 1917 (Figure 5) show the blank north wall of the transept to the east, the exact position of the "Vision of Columbus" at present. Another photograph (Figure 6) shows the hall completed with the murals installed, all except for the "Vision of Columbus", which was added at a later date. It is the only panel of the six which fits its frame tightly and whose frame has no bevel. This rather unnoticeable nonconformity is further evidence that it was added to the set. This might not have been done until 1936 at which time John Gaw Meem installed the organ on the west side of the transept. During 1981 and 1982, the murals were restored through a gift from the Agnes Tait McNulty Estate.

On the back of two of Beauregard's sketches are diagrams indicating places for his panels. Neither shows the transept of the finished Santa Fe hall; the number of panels varies from five to seven. Those panels he had sketched are marked with an "X"; the other locations are blank. Beauregard did not know the full details of the commission when he had to return from Europe and he still had in mind the commission for San Diego.

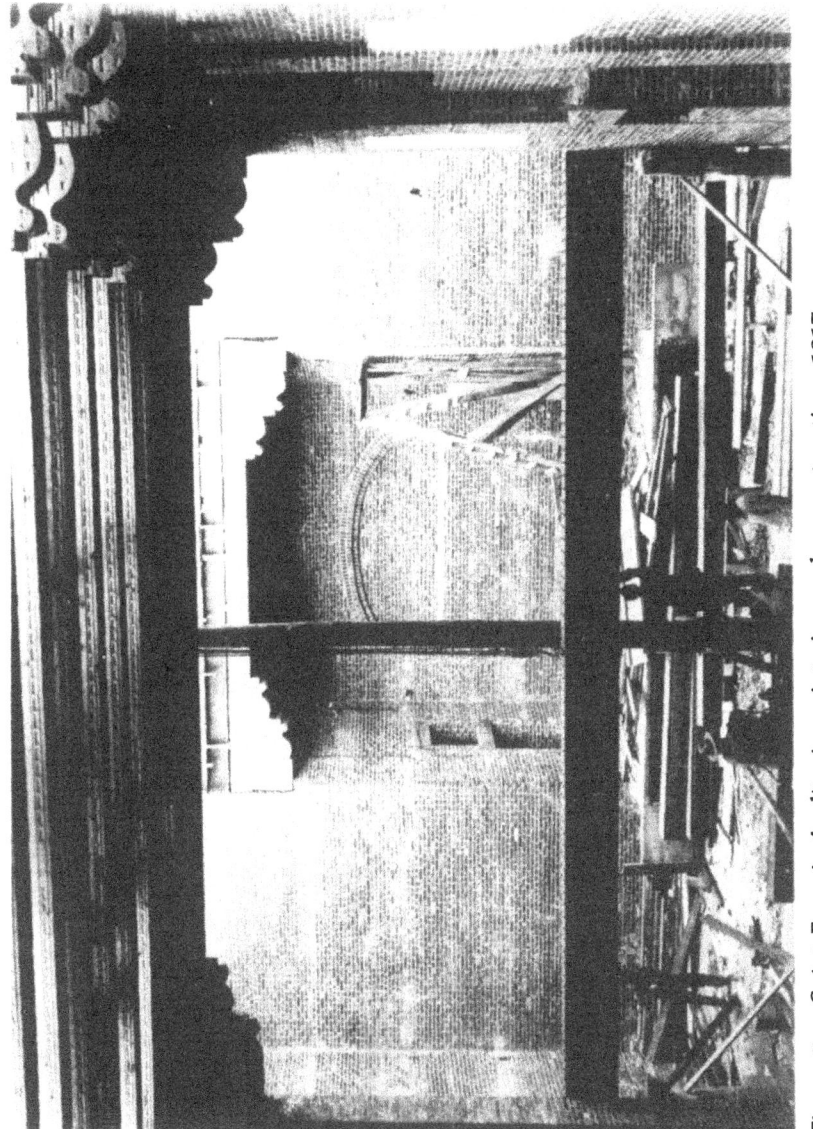

Figure 5: *Saint Francis Auditorium, interior under construction, 1917.*

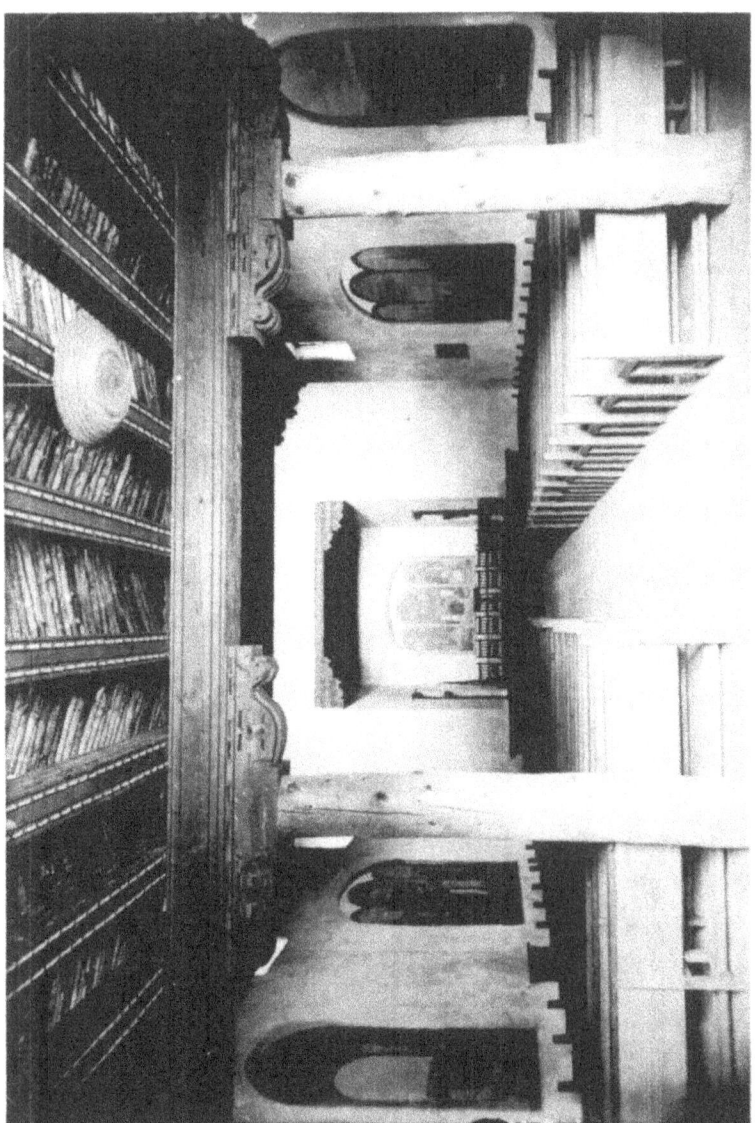

Figure 6: Saint Francis Auditorium, interior, June, 1918.

In *El Palacio*, the bulletin of the Museum of New Mexico, for 1913 and 1914, occur several reports about the mural cycle which indicate change and indecision but an unwavering dedication to the project. In the November 1913 issue is a statement of the program: "The mural paintings within the church (sic), will depict events in the life of Saint Francis of Assissi (sic), scenes of the martyrdom of the Franciscans in New Mexico, especially at Puara, near Albuquerque, and in the Revolution of 1680, in which twenty-one frayles gave up their lives for their faith." In *El Palacio*, January 1914, the program for San Diego is given as "further enhanced by the mural painting idealizing the life of Saint Francis of Assisi." In April/May 1914, *El Palacio* announced that the commission by Springer for seven canvasses "to illustrate the life and works of Saint Francis of Assisi" had been made. Beauregard's death prevented the uncompleted set of paintings from being displayed at San Diego and by then the idea of building the Museum of Fine Arts at Santa Fe was taking shape and further changes for the murals were yet to come.

No other murals in New Mexico, nor for that matter all along the eastern face of the Rockies, had shaped canvasses like those of Santa Fe. For that matter there were probably no contemporary wall decorations like these except those executed by Carl Lotave for the Museum of New Mexico, Palace of the Governors, in 1911. These were placed at cornice level in an exhibition room and were primarily landscapes. The public had access to the place he was working. A flirtation developed between the artist and the sister of Bronson Cutting, who became the most influential politician of New Mexico in the later twenties and early thirties. Hewett informed the brother of the goings-on and was flatly told to mind his own business. Lotave was not considered for the Saint Francis commission. His murals, however, still decorate the exhibition room with their views of the sites of early excavations by the Museum and School staffs. The room has been refurbished as a memorial to Jesse Nusbaum. Unfortunately, there is no notice of the artist in the room.

Mural decoration for his buildings must have signified prestige for Hewett. The question is why, since he had no western example. He had at one time been engaged in work in Washington D.C., and could have seen this type of grandiose, even bombastic, decoration visually displaying symbols and events of high importance to the nation in the capitol and elsewhere. Of more recent execution and very up-to-date were the decorations of the Boston Public Library. These gained national and international attention and made mural decoration in public buildings very popular in America.

The Boston Public Library was designed by the New York firm of McKim, Mead and White beginning in 1887 as an Italian Renaissance palace, replete with marble floors, bronze fittings and a grand staircase of munificent dimensions whose walls were covered by murals executed by the aging, world-renowned Pierre Puvis de Chavannes. His great murals for the Panthéon in Paris illustrated the life of the saviour of the city, Ste. Geneviève. For Boston, Puvis de Chavannes produced personifications set in tall, narrow panels, curved at the top, very similar to those which were to be designed for Santa Fe (Figure 7). The style of the French artist had great influence on the creation of the murals at Santa Fe.

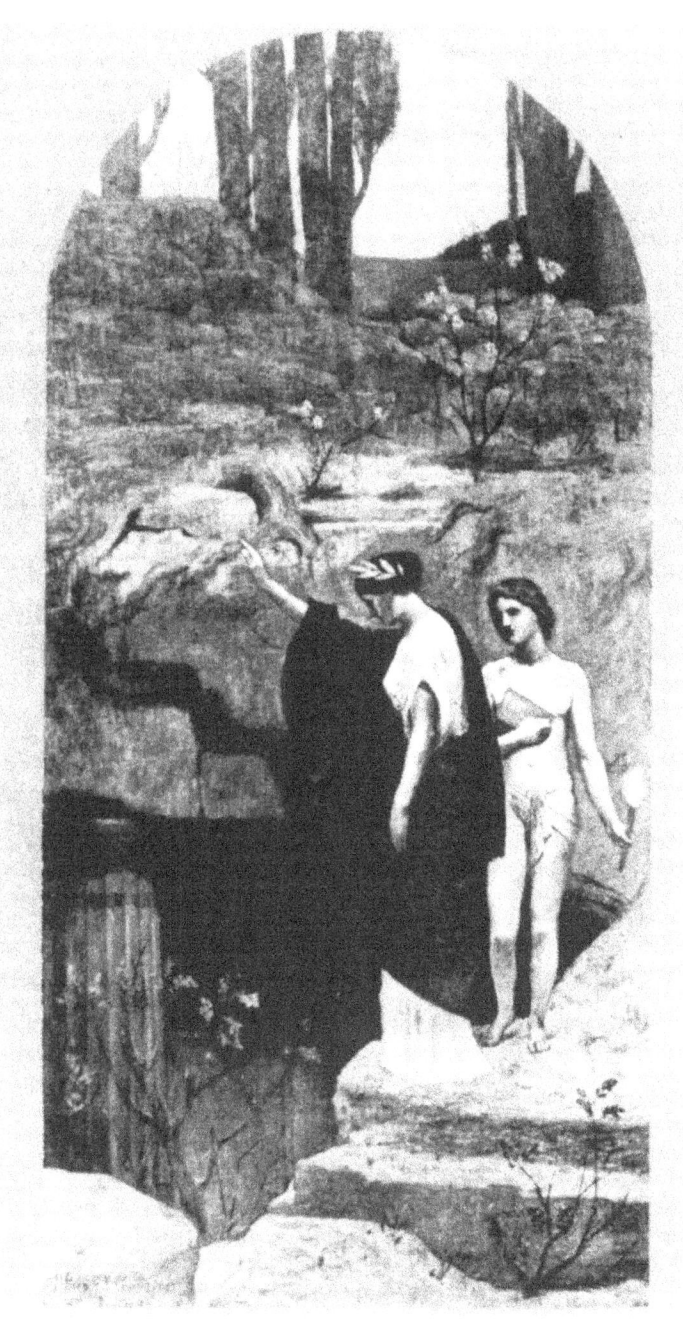

Figure 7: *"History," Puvis de Chavannes, Boston Public Library.*

It is difficult to decide whether Beauregard or someone else determined that the murals were to have Puvis de Chavannes' qualities. As will be seen in the essay on Beauregard, his letters never mention Puvis nor does his work in Europe remotely resemble that of the Frenchman. Perhaps Hewett, enamoured of the style of Puvis de Chavannes and impressed by the success of the Boston paintings gave directions, or suggestions, as to what Beauregard should do for the Santa Fe commission. At any rate, early sketches made by the artist for the first three paintings recall the dreamlike, serene settings by Puvis and the pseude-classical half unclothed figure style as well. In Santa Fe, however, the finished paintings show only one bare shoulder whereas in unblushing Paris there is a lot of nudity in the French artist's pastoral scenes.

Stanford White approached Puvis in 1891 and was met with a refusal. In 1893, however, the artist acquiesced and signed a contract for: "Les muses inspiratrices, acclament le génie, messager de lumière" (the inspiring muses, acclaim genius, messenger of light). In 1896 the paintings were installed, a date only two decades before the activity in New Mexico and time enough for the work of Puvis to have become widely famous. In Boston, other commissions were made to the great American artists, John Singer Sargent and Edwin Austin Abbey for murals in the Library. Their work was finally completed and installed by 1916 so that the authorities at Santa Fe had constantly before them the superb example of the largesse of Boston.

Difficult as was the job of delineating the subject matter of the mural cycle, it was not possible to adjust the aesthetics of the paintings to Santa Fe. It may never even have occured to those in charge. Local talent was used, and even that unproven. After the death of Beauregard, Hewett turned to those most available and therefore nearby, already involved in major undertakings for the San Diego Exposition. No standard was available to Hewett and his group to help determine what was or was not appropriate mural decoration for the Southwest. The Spanish mission churches were furnished by elaborate altarpieces with sculptures and paintings *(Figure 8)*. They must have seemed very primitive to the men of the Museum and School in 1916 and therefore unacceptable. They had not yet been made cognizant of the modern movement in art filtering into the United States from Europe. Puvis de Chavannes was the most acceptable contemporary or modern artist of whom they were probably aware. The murals of Kuaua Pueblo, now in the Coronado State Monument, had not yet been discovered, and would have been given the same oprobrious epithet — primitive. Santa Fe, however, was lucky. The murals in the auditorium can still delight as color and decoration, relieving the chasteness of the white walls of the room.

It was quite otherwise with the architectural setting of the murals. A standard which a creative architect could use was completely available in the many ruined or surviving mission churches of the State. Isaac Hamilton Rapp was encouraged to interpret the architectural past of the region and established the Santa Fe style, to the applause of Hewett, Springer, and especially Sylvanus Morley and Jesse Nusbaum, among others all of whom were agitating for the development of an architecture proper to New Mexico and its past, as distinct from California and the East. The style was a clear adaptation of the Franciscan mission buildings with some elements of pueblo architecture from the Rio Grande.

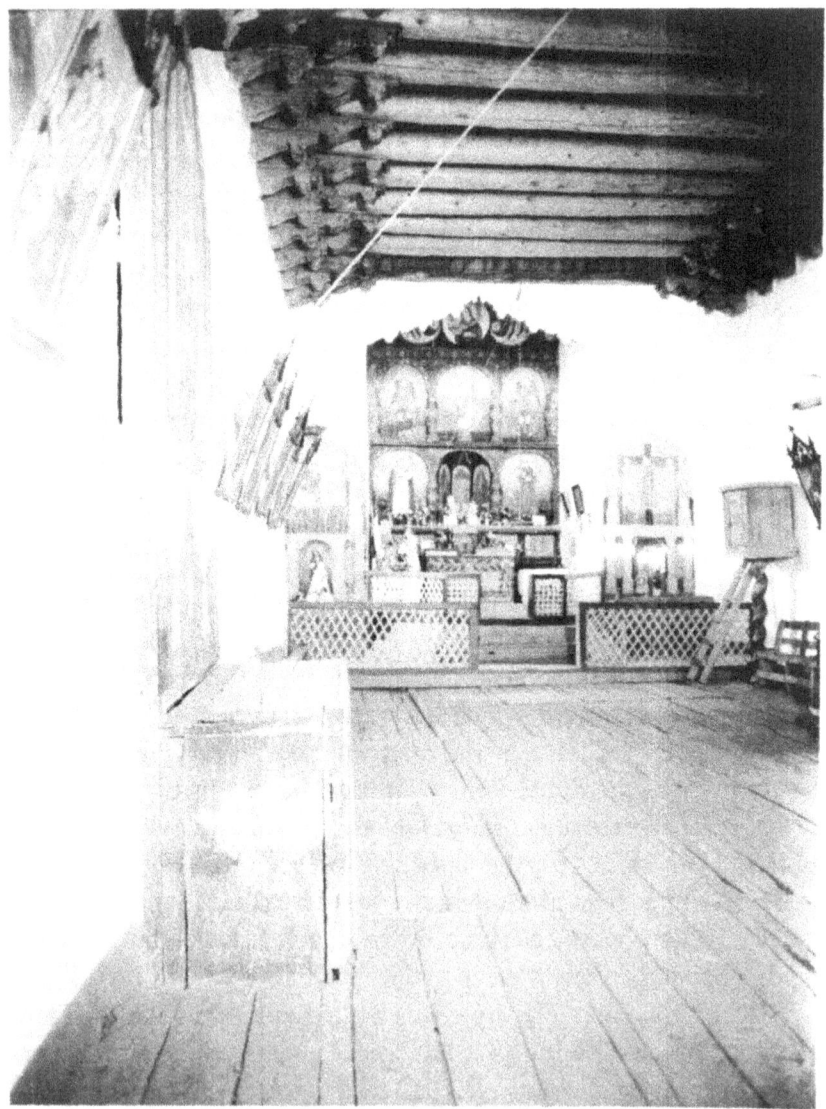

Figure 8:   *Church at Las Trampas, NM., interior c. 1935.*

Rapp approved Beauregard's plans for the murals at San Diego and eventually installed them with their niches in the auditorium of the Museum at Santa Fe. He was successful in creating a regional style whereas the murals evoked a European contemporaneity and were almost instantly out of date. Puvis de Chavannes was not Paul Gauguin, although the latter paid the former the compliment of copying his work as did Vincent Van Gogh, Picasso and others. Their message was not that, however, of Puvis whose ideal moral world was about to lose its identity through World War I.

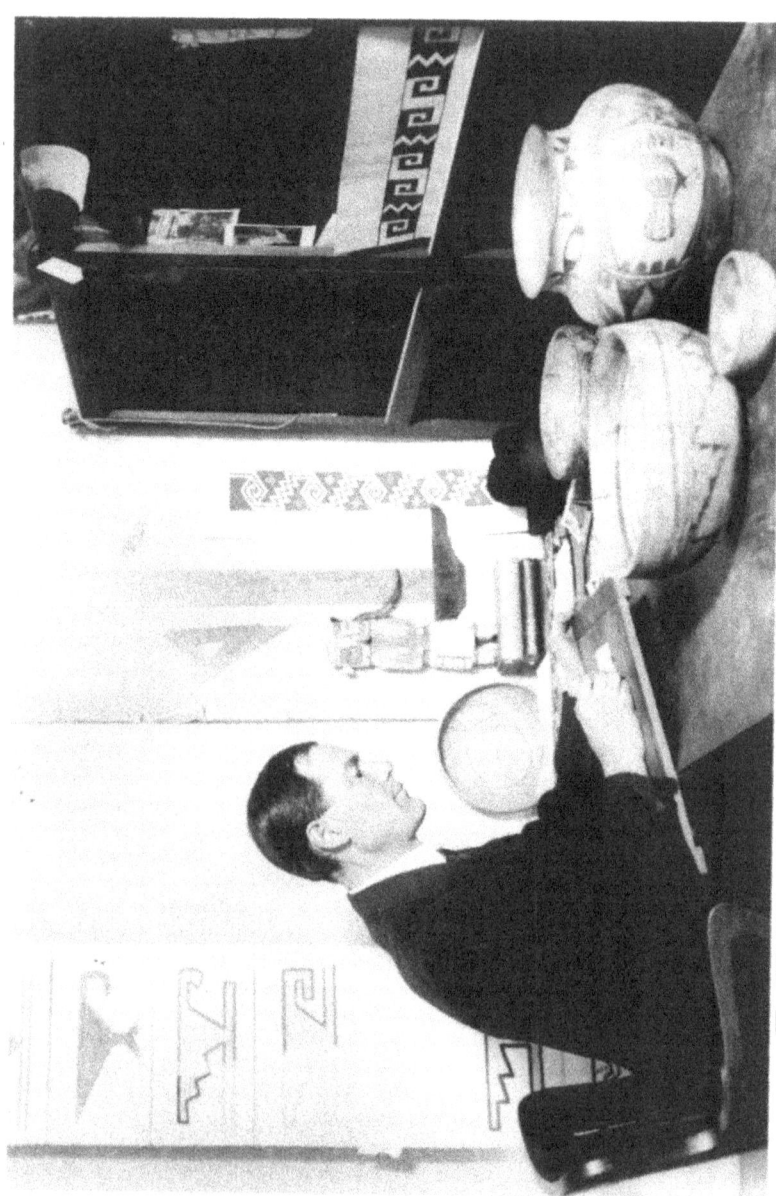

Figure 18:   *Kenneth Chapman, Office in the School of American Archeology (now Palace of the Governors), c. 1912.*

CHAPTER III

THE ARTIST

Edgar Lee Hewett preserved a great deal of his correspondence. At present, originals and copies are housed in the History Library of the Museum of New Mexico. Included in material from 1912 to 1914 are many letters by or concerning Donald Beauregard. Most of them are copies of letters Beauregard sent to Frank Springer, who was giving the artist an allowance while he pursued his studies in Europe. Copies must have been forwarded to Hewett to keep him informed of the progress of his protege. Several themes run concurrently through the correspondence; most appealing is the enthusiasm Beauregard showed for his experiences with the world of European art. Beauregard frequently speaks of financial matters, reporting costs, etc., as appropriate to his patron; consequently Springer's generosity is implied in almost every letter, along with Beauregard's recognition of his great good fortune. Lastly, there are increasing reports of ill health. Frank Springer received the following letter dated October 29, 1912, explaining who he, Beauregard, was and thanking Springer for his arrangement to assist him:

Plomanch Douarnenez
October 29, 1912

My dear Dr. Springer:
I received your letter yesterday. Under the conditions mere thanks will be far insificient (sic). I can only tell you that I am very happy in what you are doing for me and must let the

future decide if I appreciate it properly. If I make good I shall then have shown to you that I appreciate it; if I don't my thanks now are meaningless. I see no reason why I can't make good — and in a big way — for I have much physical strength, a common endowment of intelligence, and I hope, a sufficient moral strength. Your help comes at a critical moment. I was "broke". Of course it really isn't much just to be "broke". I have experienced it many times, but the point is that unless I could go on now with the work I have so nicely started perhaps I should never be able to pull myself back again. For my studies have always been full of interruptions due to financial causes. In one way it has made me what I am, but there always comes a time when interruptions must cease for a while. So I am delighted now with the thought of going on. And particularly with the prospects of later carrying on the work as you suggest at Santa Fe. It is exactly the kind of work I love. Moreover the material there is exceptional. And as I am western I feel that I am really a part of the material. I have studied considerably along archeological and social lines also, which should give me a big advantage in the future on the artistic side.

I'd think the best way will be to play out the work as we go along. I shall keep you in touch with my studies. Though it seems to me now that the quickest way and at the same time most satisfactory way to arrange it will be for me immediately upon the conclusion of my studies to go straight to Santa Fe and devote all my energies there for some time.

I shall leave here within the week for Paris. I shall take up there a strong drill in painting and drawing. I shall also do a course in Historic decoration and anatomy, and considerable reading on the outside, with the view of writing in the early spring a thesis on what I consider the logical direction of modern art. I shall correlate it with modern social conditions. To that end I shall also probably make a little trip to Holland to see the galleries there. Such is the general plan for the winter.

I know the American Express checks well. They are very satisfactory. I have found the $20.00 check the most satisfactory and shall arrange it now at that value.

And as you are helping me without much personal knowledge of my life I wonder if I shouldn't just give you an outline of it up to date. Born 1884 Fillmore, Utah, a desert town in the southern part of the state; lived on a ranch and in the saddle until 16 — having never seen a railroad until then. Left home and led almost a tramp's life for a year, roaming through mining camps, etc. Came back much wiser and started school. Entered University of Utah 1903. In 1904 represented the University at St. Louis World's Fair in the national debate there organized for state universities. Traveled the rest of the summer giving dramatic recitals throughout Utah with Prof. Babcock. Commenced to study art the same year in a tentative way. In 1906 came to Paris. Awarded first prize December, 1907 at Julian Academy for best drawing from life. In the meantime, I partly paid my way writing special correspondence for the Daily Brooklyn Eagle, Salt Lake Herald, etc. Spring of 1908 spent three months in Italy and England studying in the galleries. Most of the rest of the year did press work, cartooning and special articles for some papers. 1909-10 supervisor of art in the city schools, the High School and State School for the Deaf at Ogden, Utah. President of Teachers Assn. 1910 (200 teachers). Summers of 1909-10 was with Prof. (Byron) Cummings and Dr. Hewett in Arizona and New Mexico doing archaeology as a student (he also served as artist for the expeditions). Fall of 1910 won

State Prize for best painting under Utah Art Institute, a state institution with membership of 30 artists, all of whom have studied in Europe. I hit on a landscape which now belongs to the State Collection. Came to Spain the fall of 1911 - traveled throughout the country doing work in the galleries and came to Paris the beginning of this year. Was accepted and will hang at the national Salon this spring. Have been here at Douarnenez since June attempting to work out an individual note in my work. That, of course, takes time, but the older artists here have taken the warmest interest in me and I hope to make better reports to you later. There I am up to date. Should I excuse my financial conditon by telling you that I have sent my sister to school for four years in succession and that drained my purse.

I shall send you some snapshots of my later work when I arrive in Paris.

Most sincerely yours,
(signed)   Donald Beauregard

Another letter, this one to Dr. Hewett, is without a date but clearly is earlier than that of October 29, and shows that Hewett acted on Bearuregard's request:

My Dear Dr. Hewett -

I am writing you this time to present to you my Financial troubles. I had hoped to put it off for at least three or four months but being disappointed on some money I loaned to friends some two years ago, and depending upon them to settle with me now as they promised to do, I shall be stranded by the last of November unless help from Dr. Springer through your kindness is forth coming. I am enclosing the note, signed by Mrs. Jennie Hyde, to you which will explain the situation. That with interest would amount to about $200.00 now. I *have the greatest confidence in her as she is a very personal friend, but I have written her three times since the First of May and have received no answer.*

Besides that I have about 500 Francs ($100.00). That will last me under the conditions here in the country until about the last of November — but as I desire to leave here the First of November in order to get into school work at Paris when the season commences I should like if possible to get money by the middle of October.

And if through your confidence in me Dr. Springer can help me I shall certainly be the happiest young man in the world. As I told you when you were in Paris what I need is two solid years of study without interruption of bread earning, for I have stumbled along this far on rather a broken path and feel that unless I am helped over this particular period I might never do much worth while so far as art is concerned. I have everything in full swing now, all I need is to continue it.

Now I have figured out expenses largely on the experience of this year . . .

Beauregard continued his letter in detailing his financial matters. There is a letter to Hewett dated even earlier, March 7, 1910, in which Beauregard requests expenses for joining an expedition along the Rio Grande: "and my pencil should be particularly handy also — at least it was found so last summer". In a postscript, he added: "I am the tall red headed artist that was with Prof. Cummings last summer" (Bryon Cummings was Dean at the State University of Utah.) Other letters followed:

3 rue Vercingetorix, Paris
December 20, 1912

My dear Dr. Springer:

I am writing this to wish you a most pleasant New Year and to announce on my side some unpleasant but not too serious news. I have been feeling rather washed out for the last month or so. Last week I went to Dr. DuBouchet who is the leading American doctor in Paris and after giving me several examinations advised me to quit Paris for several months and go to a higher and sunnier climate in order to prevent any chance of tuberculosis and to regain my old standard of health. In my present physical condition, he says, I am quite open to tubercular germs, especially in the crowded ateliers of the schools. He advises a complete rest for a month — exercise, diet, etc. Now I know that I have been rather foolish. I have never given my health a moments notice and with several years without a holiday and a great deal of indoor and nervous work I have let myself run down, though all my friends say I am the healthiest looking sick man they have ever seen. Last summer was very nasty as well and I worked in a miserable damp studio eight hours a day.

And although I have to give up a fine course in anatomy and decoration I feel that I will probably gain in the long run by nipping all germs in the bud and keeping my health to the foremost. The doctor recommends Leysin, a little town quite high up in Switzerland, where accommodations are good and I can get the sun. I'll take my books and paints and shall be able to do as much work — telling work at least — as I could do in Paris. After all what an artist needs is to get into his work a highly individual note. Anyone can learn to draw and paint mechanically well, but so few ever give their work that vision which is the work of individuality. My ideas are getting well fixed now and I really believe even in my work that it will do me good to leave Paris a while. I can return in the Spring and complete my anatomy course then.

I tell you all this for fear you might think I am rather unsettled in what I want to do, etc.

I have had several artists such as Guerin, Friezo (?), Hawthorne, and Miller look at summers work and they have given me excellent criticisms. All I need is to follow up my start developing color, composition, and drawing all together.

I have been thinking that next summer I should go to Spain to paint. There is a great resemblance between our Southwest and Spain, and some more work there would help me for the work later in Southwest. Besides Zuloaga is there and his influence would be well worth while. I believe he is one of the great living painters of today. I think he is usually in Segovia.

I have not heard from Dr. Hewett recently, though he told me sometime ago that he would try to arrange some sort of scheme in regard to me and the work you suggest at Santa Fe. Most any kind of arrangement will be agreeable to me so long as I can be doing decoration with the Southwest material. And I am fully confident that I'll do it right.

There is one thing I feel, however, I am not able now to keep in touch with the Southwest feeling. I wonder if there would be any way to get hold of reports - recent reports I mean, or books recently published. I know the Smithsonian reports partly well, but anything like Matthews Navaho Legends, or the Night Chant would help me out considerably.

You can send the next installment as before to the American Express at Paris and if I need it before my return they will forward it to me.

With my very best regards,
I am, Sincerely yours,
(signed)   Donald Beauregard

Chalet de Trient, Leysin, Suisse
Janvier 8, 1913

Dear Dr. Springer:

Just a note to tell you that I am located O.K. in Leysin and find it all quite to my liking. It is surprisingly warm during the day and I have been doing some outdoor work. I can get models quite easily too and cheaper than Paris, but pension is more expensive.

I am already feeling like a new man. The air and sun together are good doctors. I went to see Dr. Raller who has a rather wider reputation in Europe for tubercular diseases and he gave me a thorough examination with the same opinion that the Paris doctor gave me that all I needed for a while is out of door life. The colds I contracted during the summer left the lungs weak. I don't cough or expectorate at all and the doctor tells me there are no adhesions, etc., but that I should be very much wiser if I kept in the outdoor life for some time instead of going back to the poison of Paris studios. And as it seems perfectly reasonable and as I can do as much or more in the open I think I shall follow his advice. After all I have had considerable academic work and now need more individual effort to work out my artistic convictions.

I shall have, I think, by the end of the month about $35.00 over the allowance, but I need some books badly and shall make an investment with it later.

I am finding the mountains very difficult subjects. Particularly at this season when they are cold and more or less colorless, but it's splended practice. The mountain types are rather rugged, interesting people and as soon as I get my bearings I shall start my figure work in earnest.

A letter addressed to the heading of my letter will reach me in safety.

Most sincerely yours,
(signed)   Donald Beauregard

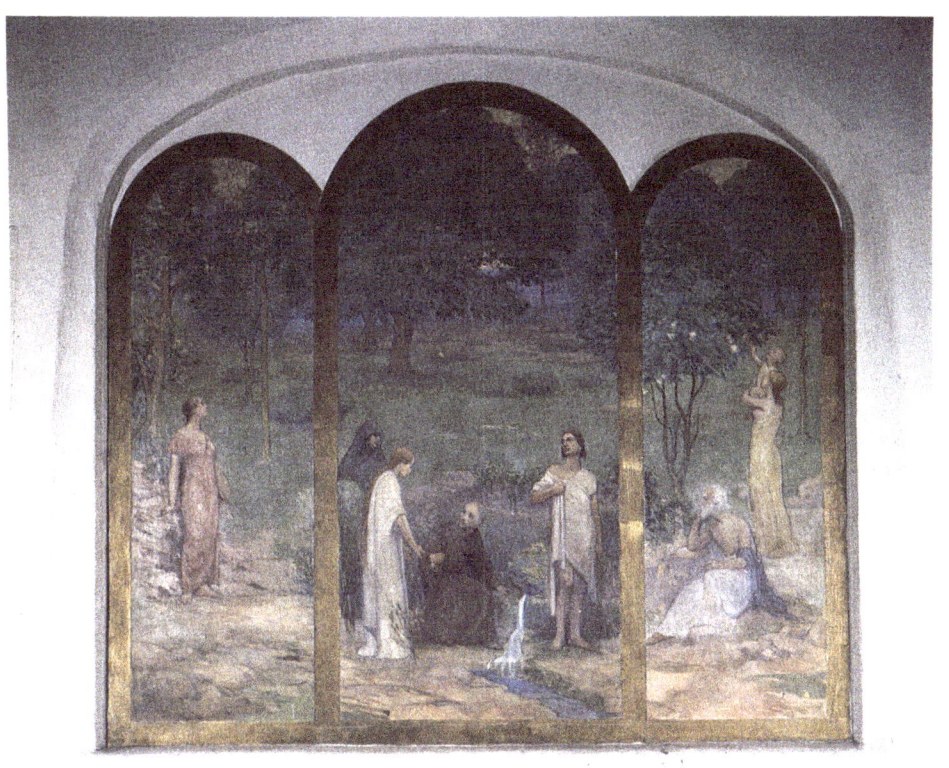

A. *"Apotheosis of St. Francis,"* St. Francis Auditorium, Santa
Fe, NM.

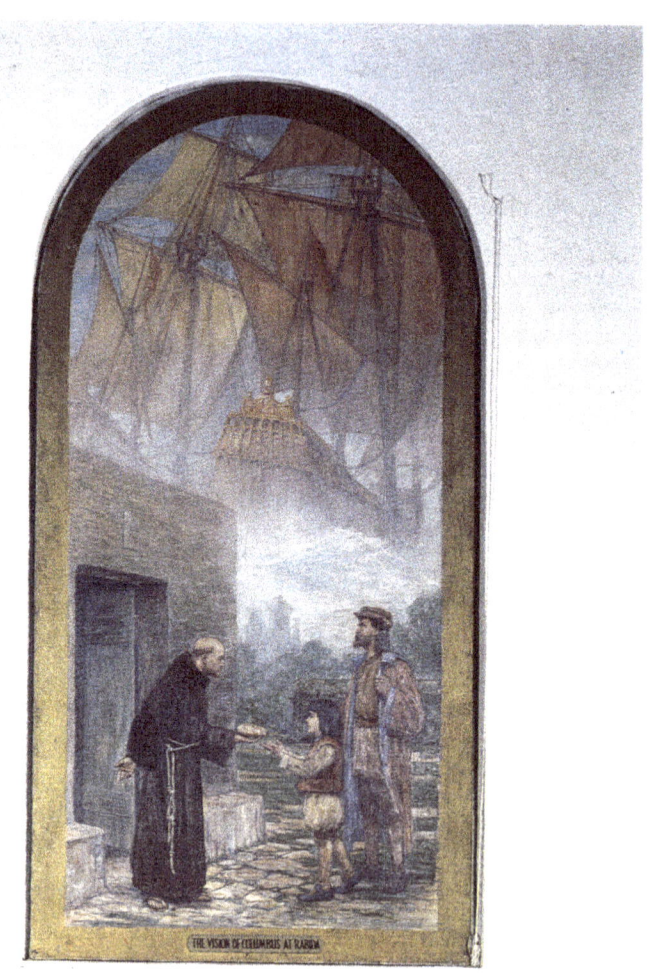

B. *"Vision of Columbus at La Rábida,"* St. Francis Auditorium, Santa Fe, NM.

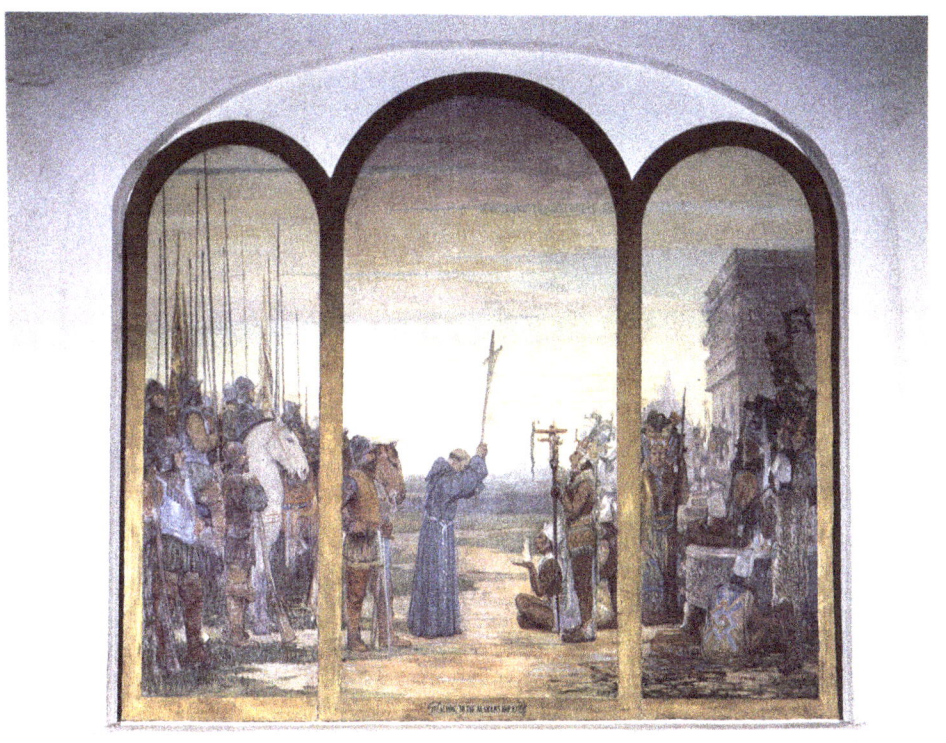

C. *"Preaching to the Mayas and the Aztecs,"* St. Francis Auditorium, Santa Fe, NM.

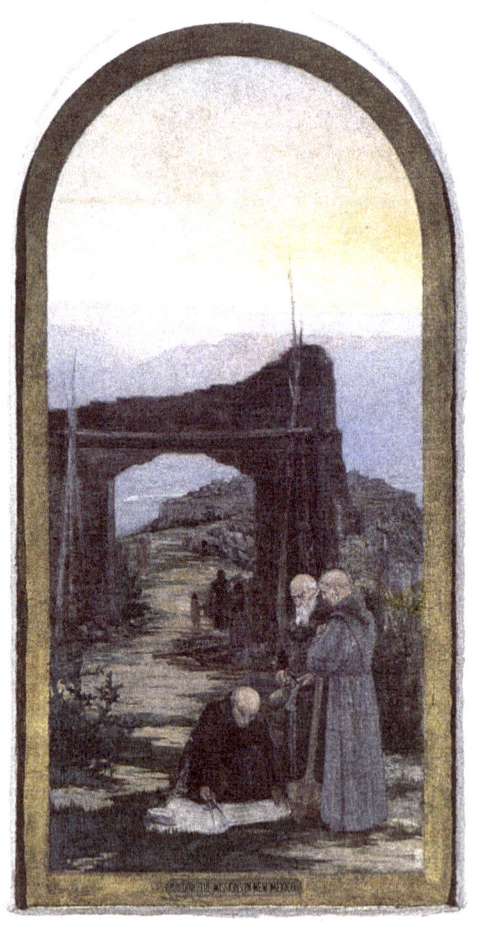

D. *"Building of the Missions in New Mexico,"* St. Francis
Auditorium, Santa Fe, NM.

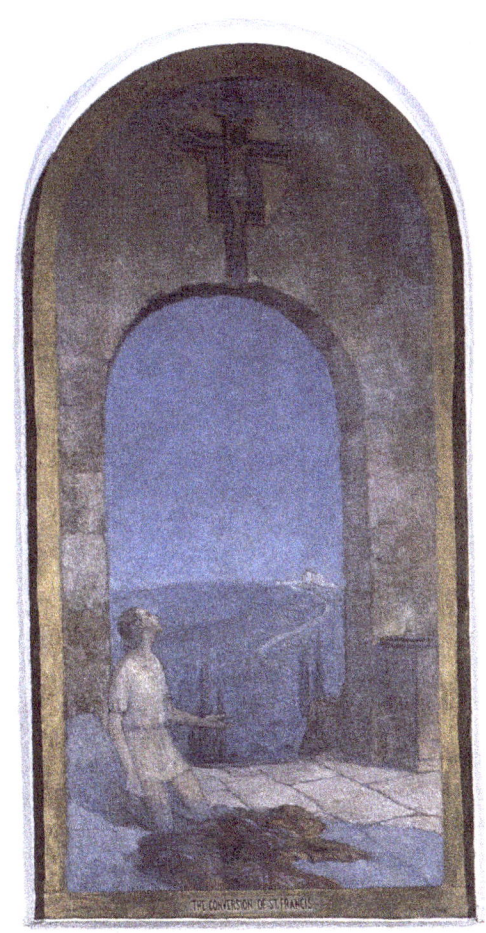

E. *"Conversion of St. Francis,"* St. Francis Auditorium,
   Santa Fe, NM.

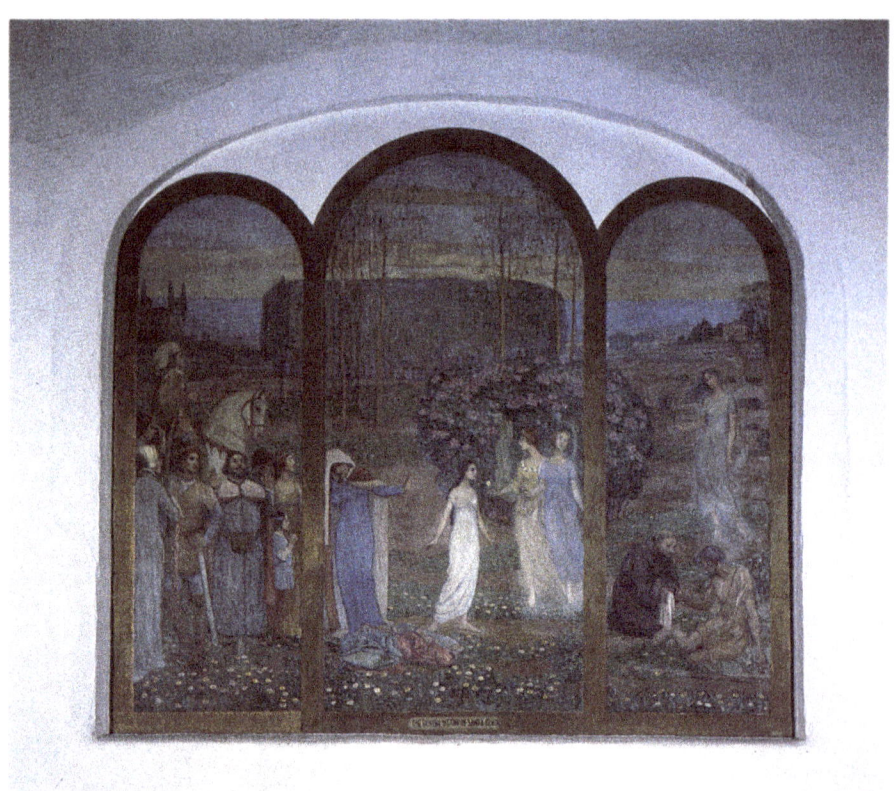

F. *"Renunciation of Santa Clara,"* St. Francis Auditorium, Santa
Fe, NM.

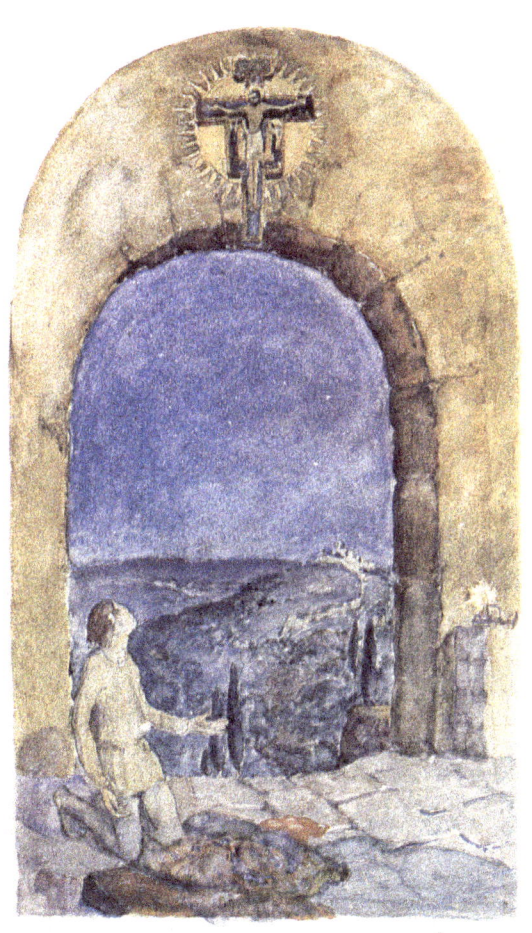

G. *"Conversion of St. Francis,"* Donald Beauregard.

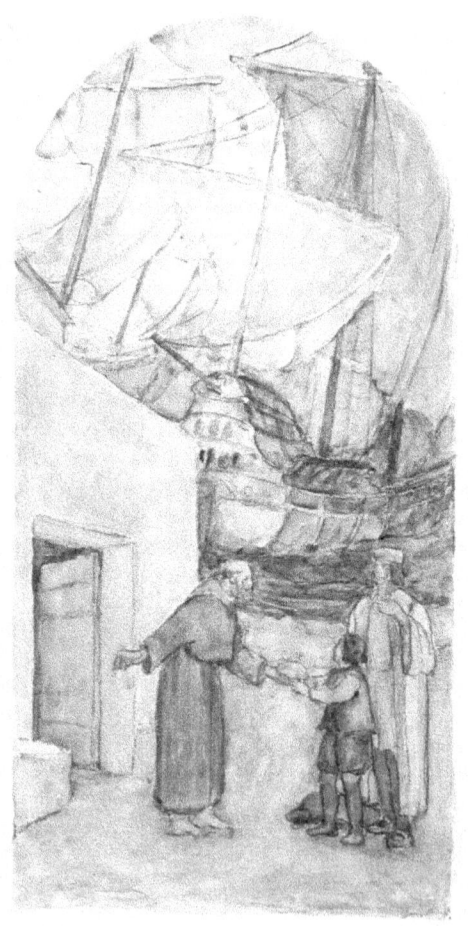

H. *"Vision of Columbus at La Rábida,"*
    Donald Beauregard.

Chalet de Trient, Leysin
April 8, 1913

My dear Mr. Springer:

You must excuse me for having attached to your name letters that don't belong there. I had always heard you spoken of as Dr. and I not sure where I found the J. I suppose it's a matter of incorrect impressions from your first letter. And although I am rather absent minded in many ways I'll try to behave in the future.

I received your letter O.K. and the annoucement of another deposit which makes the third allowance of $250.00 The American Express also wrote me yesterday that they awaited my orders for its dispersal. You can imagine how exceptionally good it seems to me to go on studying as I am now without the eternal bread question staring me in the face. Of course I know that that very problem has been a very necessary one for the development of my character, but I have tasted enough of it, I think, to appreciate now a relax in that direction. So I feel infinitely grateful to you.

I am glad to say that I believe I have at last realized something in my work that I had never found before. I told you, or meant to have told you at least that I was concentrating for a while on still life studies. I feel so encouraged about it now for I think I have expressed something that I have worked to express for sometime before without realizing. In general I believe that my ideas are rather of a primitive nature and consequently if I make my work a personal proposition I must not only express primitive ideas, but express them in a primitive way. I think I am getting at it in my still life studies now, though I have never yet expressed it either in my landscape or figure work. After a few more trys I am going to do some more figure work again and more outdoor sketching. I tried to snapshot some of my figure studies but *proved so badly that I would not think of sending them to anybody. When a picture depends more or less on color a Kodak is useless. Now the question is whether or not I shall have found myself by 1914 to take hold of decorative work of the nature which both you and Dr. Hewett have suggested to me. I certainly hope so and shall put every effort in that direction. I have written Dr. Hewett that I shall certainly want a try out at any rate. If I take it up I want to feel that I am thoroughly and definitely prepared to do something that has meaning. There is so much of that sort of work done which is useless and absolutely opposed to any aesthetic ideas of any kind. And I hope the Dr. will be able to so arrange it that whatever work is done will be done by men who are big men — thus really existing (inciting?) a sort of artistic epoch. One or two beautiful rooms are worth a hundred "pot boiled" ones. Perhaps that word "epoch" is rather a sweeping one, but possible.*

My smelling remains about the same which is a nuisance, but othewise I am in top condition and it will simply be an affair of time.

A little later I think I shall run down to Munich for a little while and ramble among the galleries and see what the fellows are doing.

> *With my best wishes and*
> *many thanks,*
> *(signed)   Donald Beauregard*

Chalet de Trient
Leysin, Suisse
May 20, 1913

My Dear Mr. Springer:

You will be interested to know that sometime ago Dr. Hewett wrote me more about the proposed plans at San Diego, and suggested that I work out a scenario for a Utah or Nevada building. I have been working on it a little these last few days and have promised him a series of sketches by the last of June. Of course, I can only send sketches and those done entirely without models as I can't find anything here that answers the purpose. The subject matter, historic and prehistoric, is very interesting to me, however, and I hope to send him what will in turn be interesting (Figure 9, sketch in the Hewett papers which might be similar to what Beauregard was able to send off). I am attempting to work out the scheme in as primitive a manner as possible — doing away with all melodramatic effects and eliminating the various "tricks" of the brush that tickle the eye. I hope later that you may see the sketches and give a perfectly frank opinion about them.

I am getting along splendidly. The doctor told me last week that I could now go where I will. I am really in tip top conditon in every way. I think though I'll stay on here for the summer. I should like to work up one or two larger canvases carried a little further than the sketches before I leave, and besides I don't know that I should find better material than right here in the village, and the other little villages close by.

When I go, however, I think Munich will be the most satisfactory place. I haven't been there yet and I want to know the various influences that are at work there. Then I should be perfecting the language at the same time, and some way I imagine the place must be more healthful than Paris. As you know Munich is one of the chief European art centers.

Most sincerely yours,

(signed)   Donald Beauregard

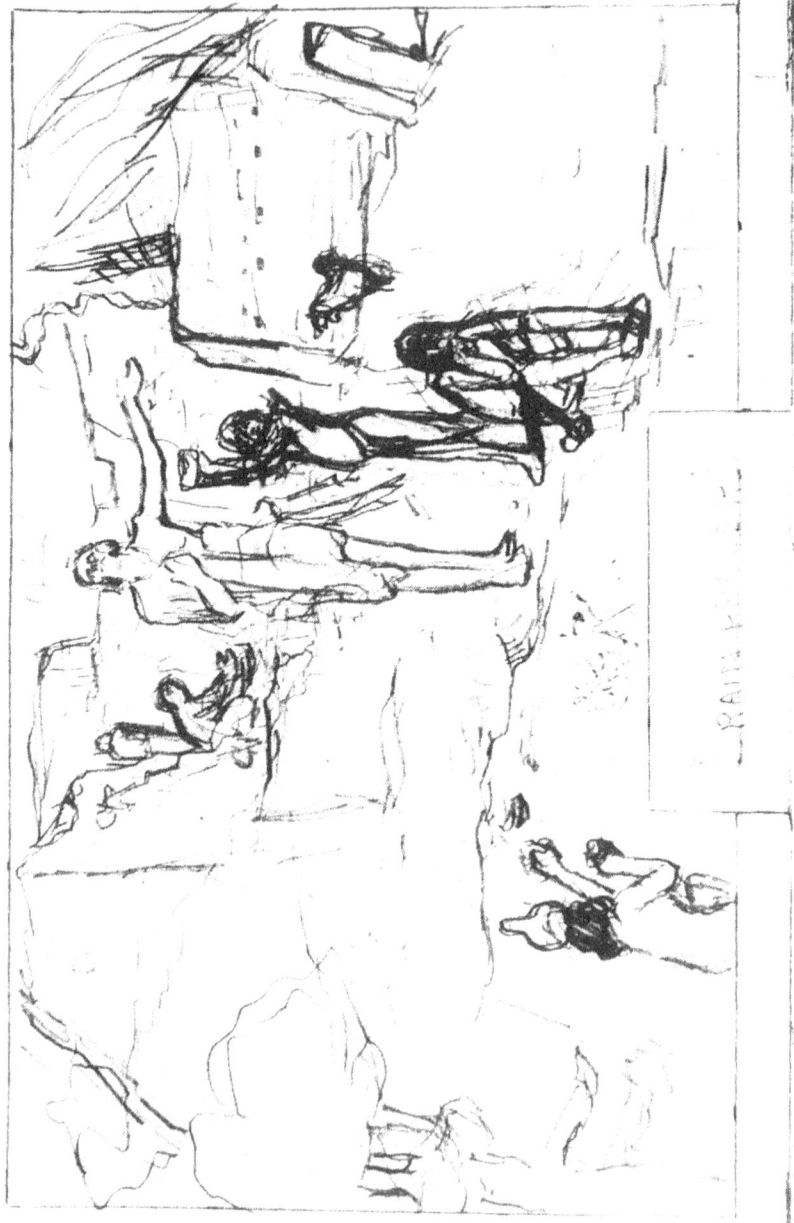

Figure 9:   *"Rain Prayer," Donald Beauregard, pencil.*

Chalet de Trient, Leysin
June 12/13

My Dear Dr. Hewett,

I shall send you Monday the promised sketches. I should send them before but that there is some red tape to go through with the consular service. I must go to Vevey and swear that I am an American etc.

I am disappointed in them. I fear you will be too. I promised more than I fear I can deliver. It is not an easy task to jump from Swiss peasants to Indians and Pioneers. But although they are nothing more or less than hurried sketches done in a medium strange to me (tempora) to facilitate posting I think they will show you that with closer proximity to the subject and more time I can do something. Due to the fact that they are worked on so small a scale I had to eliminate many details which could be included on a large scale without hurting the bigger features. You can judge them best I think by placing them 10 to 12 feet away. I have written on the back of each sketch.

I am leaving here the last of next week for Munich. I shall write you from there. I am simply bubbling over with life now.

I might add that I shall be glad to work out any details that you might suggest for any part of the decoration if I have some idea sent me of the nature of the building or buildings. As it rests now you see the evident futility of it as it is working more or less in the dark so to speak.

With my best wishes for a success of your plans.

Sincerely yours,
(signed)   Donald Beauregard

5 Ziebland Street
Munchen, Bavaria
September 12, 1913

My dear Mr. Springer:

I imagine you might be back in Washington by the time this letter reaches America so I shall address it there.

Since I last wrote you I am sorry to say that I find myself ailing again. My stomach is not properly behaving and naturally it affects my whole system. I have been to the doctors again and they call it weak digestion. So to be perfectly fair with you I have decided the best thing I can do will be to go to America immediately and put myself in condition. Here I have taken the very best care of myself. I have exercised a lot and stayed almost entirely in the open doing air work, but the summer has been rainy and damp and that doesn't seem to agree with my system. And as it is entirely unfair to you that I continue here only half a man and as I think it is the quickest way also for me to realize something in my work I had better leave Europe. I did want to stay the winter out badly for there are some things I wish to work out before I branch out into professional work, but that can be done perhaps a little later out in the southwest.

I shall leave then in a few days for Paris where my things are, take a last look at the galleries and then sail for America. I shall come to Washington and hope that I may see and talk with you there. I am very anxious to show you that I am very serious and that your confidence in me has not been misplaced. I feel now that with the knowledge I have of painting and general cultural education that I can make myself a valuable man for the work in the southwest. But, of course, I could never do that as a half invalid. At any rate if my work doesn't take on the desired shape I can turn to pedagogical ways and in a few years pay off the debt in actual money at least that I owe you. Though I wish to pay it in a bigger way.

I am behind somewhat in my allowance due to doctor bills and what I call expensive Munich. Could you then kindly send me another allowance upon receipt of this letter and as soon as I get it I shall arrange to sail. The sooner I go the better, I think, though I presume it would cost too much to telegraph the amount.

My present idea is to go directly to my old home where of course I can live for practically nothing and get the care that only a mother can give. There I shall simply throw off all studies for about three months and do real manual work in the open field. I am sure in that way soon to be perfectly strong again. After I shall be ready to go at any kind of work that you or Dr. Hewett may suggest in the southwest, and ready to give it my undivided attention. But we may talk this over, with your permission, when I come to Washington.

It might interest you to know that I have found lately considerable inspiration among the modern Munich painters. Their work which at first seems rather formal and uninviting grows on one, particularly among the decorations. Such men as Erler and Putz have certainly worked out some very interesting sides of modern decoration. It had a boldness and definiteness that carries conviction, though often weak in the finer more aesthetic sentiments. It has been rather a good influence for me to be under after so much of the French. I think the greatest inspiration outside of Valesquez at the Prado in Madrid I have had was the other day at Scheissheim just north of Munich where I saw the work of Hans Maries (Hans von Marees?). He was a spirit that lived apart something on the order of Rembrandt though more a decorator. His deep tones of color and their varied movements and juxtapositions give me the same feeling that I have had when I hear the 9th Symphony of Beethoven. Unhappily reproductions are hard,

or next to impossible to get hold of, but I hope sometime that
we might talk over just such things for I feel that you must
have a love for art or you would not be willing to support so
much its growth.

   Excuse my ramblings and believe me,
                    Sincerely yours,
                    (signed)   Donald Beauregard
                    11 Rue Scribe
                    Paris, France
P.S. I shall await your advice before sailing though the sooner
I go the better it will be all around.

   In the mid-twenties there was some question as to the proper
disposal of the estate left by Donald Beauregard, particularly
the paintings, sketches, and drawings that were in Santa Fe.
Some of those who had been present in 1913-14 wrote down
their recollections of that time. Following is the statement of
Kenneth M. Chapman, dated April 28th, 1925.

   During the years 1913 and 1914 I was employed by Mr.
   Frank Springer in research work, which I carried on, prin-
   cipally in the Museum of New Mexico in Santa Fe. During
   that time, as for many years previous, I attended to certain
   business matters for him, in addition to my regular work.

   Donald Beauregard came to Santa Fe in the fall of 1913, to
   work on a series of mural paintings. He spent a month or
   more in arranging a studio at the Museum and in supervising
   the making of frames, stretchers, etc., for his paints. He
   began painting about December first and kept at it until later
   February, 1914, when his illness began to interfere with his
   work. In March his condition became worse, and he decided
   to go to Denver for an examination. He told me on leaving he

expected to return within two weeks and that he had left most of his belongings in his room.

Later, I received a letter from him, written in Denver and stating that he would be obliged to go to his home in Utah, and asking me to attend to the disposition of his property left in his room and in his Museum studio. I attended to the packing and shipment of the articles which he wished to be sent to his home. He further directed me, as Dr. Springer's agent, to pack his paintings, sketches, photographs, prints, and books and art magazines in certain boxes and a wicker trunk which could be locked, and to store them at the Museum subject to Mr. Springer's order. He added that he wished Mr. Springer would look over his books and magazines when he returned from Washington and that he would be glad to have them sent to him if Mr. Springer did not care particularly for them.

I followed his directions, and advised Mr. Springer of the matter, and received his reply stating that Beauregard had written him to the same effect.

(signed) Kenneth M. Chapman
Santa Fe, NM

School of American Archeology
Museum of New Mexico
Santa Fe, New Mexico
February 10, 1914

Dear Mr. Springer:

Your letter, check and photos came several days ago. I have waited to write in order to send you the photographs Jesse (Nusbaum) took of the sketches. Someway he doesn't get at it to finish them, but I shall send them as soon as I get them.

I have also, with the exception of some retouching or going over, completed the first small panel the sketch of which you saw. Chap and the rest seem to think it goes pretty well. I turned it out in a week — a little less. I figure that I must complete the next triple panel by the 10th of May and another by the last of June — then I shall pull out O.K. I have the first of the triple panels well under way and if I don't have too much trouble getting models I shall go right ahead with it. I admit that so far I have only found one or two models that are interesting, but the ladies are looking for others. I can't find a good St. Francis. I shall probably have to hire some men models a little later.

All the stretchers are made at last. They are good solid ones and it took 148 1/2 hours to make them which at 50 cents per hour — $75.25. Two rolls of canvass, which is about half enough for the whole series, cost $50.40. For paints and different small material $39.65. And I must send again for some more white soon. The Seligman Hardware Co. bill is $27.10. Now part of that, as you will see, is for blinds, etc. for the studio, but that I suppose I must let go as the Museum paid the lumber bill and the hardware bill at Santa Fe Hardware Co. Those I think are all the big items which amounts to $191.40.

That seems like a big expense particularly since I have had to expend really a good many dollars on a lot of little things outside of those items. But of course now there will be practically no expense except for the balance of the canvass. Unhappily I can not get canvass that will answer the purpose unsized. Otherwise it would be about 1/3 the price I have to pay and really better canvass.

I have been thinking over the placing of your head on one of the figures and have decided that it fits preeminently the head for philosophy. My only difficulty there is that it will be almost impossible to use a profile to suit the head. Possibly however I can rearrange the figure to suit the head. The photo with the hand on the face appeals to me as being pretty good, and that could be used with the figure as it really is. I shall take the best of care of the photos. I think I shall write Mr. Hodge for some photos of himself. You are right, his head is strong. etc., etc.,

(signed)   Donald Beauregard

School of American Archaeology
Museum of New Mexico
Santa Fe, New Mexico
March 6, 1914

My dear Mr. Springer:

I have a disagreeable bit of news for you on which I shall appreciate your advice. It concerns my health. For some time I have been having a bad time again with my stomach. I have quit the hotel and have been dieting by myself — breakfast and luncheon at the studio for several weeks past, but apparently to no avail. In the meantime, a swelling which I *noticed last summer when my stomach was bad, at the base of my neck has been growing rapidly lately until I can hardly wear an ordinary shirt. Today I went to Dr. Massie and he immediately pronounced it a cystic goiter (spelling?) and recommended that I be operated upon right off, as it could and would most probably grow to dangerous proportions. He said the stomach trouble was most probably closely connected with it, in fact a result of it, and that it would be impossible for me to properly work in such a condition. I sleep but little and am, I hate to admit, soon tired out. Now I don't like the idea of the knife at all, but Dr. Massie assures me that that is the only remedy. He himself knows nothing about goiter operations and advises that I go to Mayo Brothers at Rochester, Minn., where I would be assured of a quick operation. He says that I need not stay there more than 10 days and then be ready for work again.*

I'd told him that at all odds I wanted to finish the big triple panel before I left which will take about three weeks or perhaps a little less.

I have it well under way and as I feel that it is going successfully I want to finish it right off. I think in fact that it is much better than the original sketch promised. I have changed it in many places and it makes a better decoration.

Will you give me your advice? Do you think there is any way out of it other than an operation? Of course if I can get through with it in a couple weeks and then back to work with renewed energy why then I can carry the whole plan through without difficulty even working only half days. The present Santa Clara panel you see has more figures than any of them and the figures are what takes the time.

(signed)   Donald Beauregard

Kindly drop me a note.

St. Luke's Hospital
Pearl Street between 19th and 20th Aves.,
Denver, Colo.
March 18th, 1914

Dear Mr. Springer:

Just a note to say that I am O.K. I was operated at the stomach Saturday. The doctor found a glanular growth under the stomach not in it which he has sent to the Pathologist for examination. Outside of gas in rather large quantities I have gotten on fine. The gas is going now and I shall soon be ready for the neck work. Doctor seems to think it might be like the stomach — a glanular trouble and not goiter. I am well cared for and quite comfortable.

With kindest regards,
(signed)   Donald Beauregard

St. Luke's Hospital
Pearl Street between 19th and 20th Ave.,
Denver, Colo.
March, 27, 1914

My dear Mr. Springer:

At last a definite decision has been reached about me. I am sorry to tell you it is not a happy one. I have waited to write until now in order to put it before you plainly. I told you the Pathologist had taken the mass from the stomach for examination, and finally he sent the report that it is cancer. I can't tell you the scientific name, but it shows two kinds of cancerous growth both of which, says Dr. Perkins, are bad. Now that seems to upset about as much as anything can the plans that we have developed about my work, etc. The doc-

tor insists that I immediately begin to lead the simple life in the open with every advantage for proper diet and exercise without strain in order to resist as much as possible the blood determination that naturally results from cancer. He has not set any limit as to how long a chap might live. He only says — get to fighting. Naturally a fellow wants to hang on as long as possible and so I am forced to think now that the best plan for me will be to hike for home where I shall have a mother's care and every advantage fighting.

It is a pretty thick veil to hang over a fellow, but I am not a baby. I have met too many disagreeable things long before now to whimper. In fact, so far as I am concerned I don't care a straw, but I do care perhaps on your account more than any other, and of course for my parents also and family. You have been so extremely liberal (Springer was footing the hospital bill) in all ways and have expressed so much confidence that I shrink before the thought of not being able to show my appreciation for it. I started out brave enough, as I think the canvass there at Santa Fe will show, but even that is unfinished. I tried hard to finish it, but I really didn't have the strength. I couldn't possibly go on with it just now at least, and the doctor thinks I had better not try as I would only pull down instead of up. But some way or other, it seems to me, the work ought to be carried out. New Mexico had counted on it. Of course, it would be difficult to get anyone who would care to, or who could develop the plans as already conceived, unless perhaps Mr. Parsons (Sheldon Parsons who became a successful artist of the Santa Fe scene) of New York whom I have known here at Santa Fe since my arrival, could be induced to take it up. He is not strong — has weak lungs, I believe — but he has watched the work since it began, is in sympathy with it and from the sketches I have seen him do I should say he could do it better than anyone else. It's an idea which comes to me merely at the moment.

I hope you won't see too much cowardness on my part in the matter. But I am really without strength now. Perhaps by the end of the summer I shall be stronger. Certainly I shall fight it. And if I am I shall be very glad indeed to push it through. Couldn't you drop me a night telegram of advice?

With kindnest regards,
(signed)   Donald Beauregard

School of American Archaeology
Museum of New Mexico
Santa Fe, New Mexico

April 7, 1914

Mr. Frank Springer
National Museum
Washington, D.C.

My dear Mr. Springer:

I have been waiting for news about Mr. Beauregard but as yet have no word since a week ago today when I left Denver. The fact that he has not written to me makes me apprehensive that he did not make as satisfactory recovery from the effects of the operation as we hoped he would for he promised to send me a line just as soon as he was able to write and the doctor thought that would be only three or four days. I have written to him and Dr. Perkins also asking for further information and word may possibly come within a day or two. Unfortunately I have to leave in the morning so it may be several days yet before I can send you any new information.

As I think it all over and study the conditions as disclosed by Dr. Perkins' examinations and operation I must say it looks to me virtually beyond hope. I do not see how there can be but one result unless something little short of miraculous occurs.

Going over Mr. Beauregard's work here I am greatly impressed with its value. I really had no conception of it before. Taking it altogether his work in oil, water-color, charcoal and pencil sketches, etc., it makes a fine showing and really represents very fully the development of Beauregard from the time he made those first sketches while with us out at the Rito (now Bandelier National Monument). It illustrates well the different art influences that he came under during his sojourn in Europe and through all of it you see developing his own individual power.

All this makes me feel that his work should be kept together. It would be a pity to have it scattered about among his friends and relatives as it probably might be. Accordingly in writing him freely the other day with reference to his unfinished work here as well as other matters that I felt he ought to consider, I made the suggestion to him that his work should if possible be kept together and that in view of the interest you had taken in his career he might like to direct that all his art work be turned over to you. My thought was that in case this should be done you might like to have us put it in good shape for exhibition, providing port-folios, frames, etc. and installing it in a room to itself. This might be, for the present, the studio that we prepared for him, and later on some other disposition could be made of the collection. I hope that the suggestion commends itself to him and to you.

I have also given considerable thought to the matter of the unfinished work for the New Mexico building. It would of course be a great satisfaction to everybody concerned and most especially to Mr. Twitchell, if the paintings could be finished and installed in the building as Planned. However, the plan is too good a one and the compositions as developed too fine to justify taking chances with. As the paintings are destined eventually for our building here I would much rather see the work entirely suspended until we felt absolutely certain that we could put it through about as successfully as we originally hoped to. I seriously thought some days ago of suggesting that Mr. Parsons, whom I believe you met here, might be engaged to finish the work with Mr. Chapman's assistance, but I am less favorable to that plan now. I have had some talk with him about the matter and I must say that he has as yet not furnished me with convincing evidence that he could do it properly. As I go over those compositions for the St. Francis panels I feel that we worked out something better than we at the time realized and the task of taking these up where Beauregard left off and carrying it out in all is possibilities might be better in some ones hands who was familiar with the work. It is one to be most seriously considered.

I will tell you what my best judgment in the matter is at this moment, though you will of course not regard it conclusive at all. It is merely what I arrived at after thinking the matter over for some days and considering it in every possible aspect. I may change my mind about the matter and very probably a better solution may occur to you. My present thought is that: Mr. Vierra is back now and his Central American work has been most satisfactory. I feel certain that his job is to be completed in a highly satisfactory manner. It will take him until some time in the Fall. By that time we will doubtless know the out-come as to Mr. Beauregard. Meanwhile Chapman will be going east soon and perhaps after his work with *you is finished he might go on up to New York and take special work as a preparation for this particular thing. Then he and Vierra together might take up the St. Francis painting and giving it all the time necessary, perhaps finish it more nearly in the spirit of the original idea than could be done by a person unfamiliar with it.*

It is possible that they might finish it so that it could be installed in the New Mexico Building during the last half of 1915. I wish you would consider this idea and let me know what you thnk of it. I will be leaving from New Orleans on the 16th of this month and perhaps you could send a line at the St. Charles Hotel at New Orleans that I could have before leaving.

Everything is going well about the institution and prospects are good for our Summer Session.

> *With sincere regards, I am,*
> *as always Faithfully yours,*
> *(signed)   Edgar L. Hewett*

ELH-z

> *Filmore, Utah*
> *April 19, 1914*

My dear Mr. Springer:

I am at last home and am feeling considerably better for it, although you may imagine it was a rather difficult trip to get out of bed and travel two nights and a day on the train and another whole day in a coach or buggy over 40 miles of muddy desert road. It upset my stomach fearfully, but cleaned me out so thoroughly that now my appetite is greatly improved. It is fine to be home and have a parent's care, although things of course are not convenient as in a hospital. I am fully expecting to pick up right along. At the hospital the atmosphere grew pretty pessimistic and I was losing, rather than gaining.

With my deepest regards,
(signed)   Donald Beauregard

May the Thirteenth
1914

My Dear Mr. Springer:

Your several letters have been received and I think we are virtually of one mind with reference to the work so sadly broken up by the death of Mr. Beauregard which was a tragedy, and which appears all the more callamitous when one studies the work that he had underway. It is clear that none of us have over estimated it. The subject looms deeper the more one thinks of it, and Beauregard was rising to it with great power.

But there is nothing one can do in a reverse like this, except to take up another notch in his belt and go ahead. Beauregard has left a truely valuable collection of paintings. I have arranged in the Studio the Saint Francis scheme, so that it can all be seen at a glance, and in a careful selection of his best things it makes a very pleasant room, and one that will only be shown to those who have some particular reason for wishing to see it. All the rest of his works I have stored in a little room back of the studio that is being now used entirely as an art store room, and which is always under lock and key.

Your wish as to the completion of the Saint Francis plan is exactly my own. If Chapman can stretch up to it nothing could be finer, and there is no doubt in my mind but that he and Vierra can at least do it as a joint work.

I am now very well posted concerning the work of Mr. Parsons. He has had about a dozen of his pieces on exhibiton here during the last two weeks. His work is greatly lacking the strength and originality that was coming out so remarkably in Beauregard's. In this I find that my view is shared by those here in town who are best qualified to judge. Among others, Mrs. Rapp feels that it would be a great mistake to let him undertake to finish the work, moreover his health is precarious, and we think we should take no further risk in that line.

Vierra's stock is going up at an amazing rate. His Quirigua panel (for the San Diego Exposition) leaves all his former work far behind. I have never before admitted that any thing else we have brought out here has approached the work of Lotave's, but now I do not hesitate to say that Lotave's match has arrived. I predict that when you see this Quirigua Painting you will say that Vierra need not "take off his hat" to the greatest of them. His trip to Guatemala did him a vast amount of good. His composition of the Quirigua ruins is, etc., etc., etc.

.   *(signed)   Edgar Lee Hewett*

Following is an excerpt from a letter, dated May 5, 1914, Fillmore, Utah, from Lilian Beauregard to Frank Springer:

We know you to be a very special friend of his. Your kind letter he opened and read and strong, calm man that he was sobs shook his body and we left him alone for a few minutes since we knew he did not like to have one see the emotion he could not conceal. After a time he said to Mother "I have friends that are so valuable and so good to me that it hurts. They are all so good to me that it touches me so."

"We had him home just two weeks and a day."

Beauregard died on May 2, 1914 and it is poignant to realize that most if not all the letters to Springer were written to a man Beauregard had never met. The letters appear sincere, positive, almost naive in their enthusiasm. They are devoid of all reference outside the personal relations between patron and protege, outside observations concerning things and events impinging on Beauregard's pursuit of art in Europe. A letter extant in the collection of the History Library which was written to one of Beauregard's contemporaries in the Hewett entourage, Neil Judd, is dated April 3, 1913, from Leysin:

> I have just finished Perrot's Egyptian Art. Of course I don't take it up the way you do. I read more or less promiscously (sic) as a thoroughly good Bohemian should!
>
> No I didn't hear about the Inaugural Reception etc. I am thoroughly isolated here. I read the French papers of course but I haven't seen an English or American paper for 8 or 9 months. I am sadly behind the times. I live pretty much in the clouds — especially here as we are about 6000 ft. high. Besides I am trying to work out this paint proposition and that takes a chap almost out of earth. To be able to paint academically is more or less an easy task but to put something special in ones work requires a certain "cloud life" for awhile anyway. I have gone through all sorts of methods and have followed all modern tendencies and now I am trying for something that is nothing but "Beauregard" and I find it darned hard to be perfectly honest though little by little I feel that I am getting at something half way respectable.
>
> etc., etc.

The letter is of interest because it enables us to control our reading of Beauregard's correspondence with Springer and Hewett. It is less formal but not much so. He does show some humor and joshing and friendship not only with Judd but with the others of the group such as Morley, to whom he sends greetings.

There is an unexpected difference between the paintings and sketches Beauregard did in Europe and those executed at Santa Fe, particularly those of the Alpine landscapes and the byways of Tuscan Italy. The latter have, at least in their technical approach, a much broader, less defined, more atmospheric manner than do the murals in the auditorium. Of the artists in Europe he mentions, each had a manner approaching his own, from Zuloaga to Hans von Marées (?). He does not seem to have been attracted to Puvis de Chavannes in Paris or to the Symbolists in Brittany. The French influence so clear in the Saint Francis murals must be the result of Hewett's and therefore Springer's requests. If so, Beauregard certainly painted to satisfy his patrons.

CHAPTER IV

FINISHING THE MURALS

Kenneth M. Chapman had known Edgar Hewett for a relatively long time. Hewett had appointed him instructor of art at the Territory of New Mexico, Las Vegas Normal School in 1899. In his turn Hewett had been selected as President of the Normal School through the efforts of Frank Springer who had become acquainted with him through their mutual interests in the anthropology and the archeology of the Southwest. Chapman had been born in 1875 in Indiana and as a youth worked in engraving shops in Milwaukee, Chicago, and Saint Louis. In 1899, he moved west as did so many others to Las Vegas, New Mexico, for reasons of health. He worked at both Las Vegas and at Santa Fe under Hewett and in between assignments helped Frank Springer in Washington. He was in Santa Fe and saw to the administration of the School and Museum while Hewett was away in Central America and later at San Diego.

Chapman was a natural choice for Hewett and Springer to finish the Saint Francis murals since he had been familiar with Beauregard and with the project from its beginning. He proved a good choice. So far as known, however, he received no special help in preparing for the assignment.

Chapman was fascinated by Native American crafts, particularly pottery of the Pueblos of the Rio Grande. He spent untold hours, meticulously copying motifs from the pots that came into his hands and eventually published three volumes of the designs, a compendium of hundreds and hundreds of carefully and sharply drawn units. His interest in Pueblo pottery eventually led to the foundation in 1923 of the Pueblo Pottery Fund, succeeded in 1925 by the Indian Arts Fund. The success of these endeavors and his training under Hewett made him persona grata to the John D. Rockefeller, jrs. when the latter founded the Laboratory of Anthropology in 1927 at Santa Fe. Jesse Nusbaum became Director of the new institution and Chapman took up an appointment there. The new foundation and the appointment of two of his most useful assistants must have astounded and humiliated Hewett for a while. Neither Nusbaum nor Chapman had Hewett's ability to raise money and the Laboratory did not prosper.

Chapman belonged to the period of anthropology which was interested in description and inventory. He probably knew more about Southwest pottery than anyone else. However, he was not given to flights of fancy. For that reason he was excellent for the Saint Francis mural project; he would follow Beauregard's sketches faithfully and hence the program as already established. This he did most ably. He apparently was very proud to be associated with the project. In a brief biographical catalogue entry (now on file in the Library of the Museum of Fine Arts) Chapman listed himself as follows: Born: Ligonier, Ind. 1875, resident of New Mexico since 1899. Painter: water color, pen and ink. Style: realistic. Studied: Art Institute of Chicago; Art Students League, N.Y. Represented: murals in Saint Francis Auditorium, Museum of New Mexico. Illustrator and author; authority on Indian art.

Much the same kind of interest in anthropology was to motivate the field work of Sylvanus Morley, another Hewett recruit. His life work was Mayan archeology and one of his great contributions to Mayaology was a catalogue of Mayan glyphs. He was also willing to venture beyond the collection of material and published a most influential synthesis of information about the Maya. He joined Hewett first, from Harvard, for a summer field trip of archeological exploration in the Southwest. He followed Hewett to Santa Fe and took part in the former's expeditions to Quiriqua, Honduras, in 1910 and 1911. Perhaps because of his participation in the activities of the School of American Archeology under Hewett, Morley became convinced by the Pueblo natives of the essential peacefulness of their culture. He assigned parallels between the crafts and the personal characteristics of the New Mexico Pueblo Indians and the Maya of Central America. It is only very recently that Mayaologists have rejected his theories about the Old Kingdom Maya and have succeeded in deciphering the language of the glyphs and arrived at a more realistic, even bloody, image of Mayan society.

The belief that the Pueblo Indians and the Maya had a great deal in common certainly was fostered in the circle around Hewett at Santa Fe. One result is definitely the presence of the Maya in the Saint Francis mural cycle. In the triptych concerning the conversion of the natives of the New World, the Maya were selected as representing the inhabitants of New Mexico. There is an interesting cross-influence among the members of the School and Museum at Santa Fe. Morley was probably not aware of how his attitude towards the Maya was formed, partially of course at Santa Fe. In his turn he was most active and emphatic in support of the development of the Santa Fe style, including the portal of the Palace of the Governors and the New Mexico building at the San Diego Exposition. At the end of his career, Morley returned from Yucatan to Santa Fe to assume the directorship of the School of American Archaeology. Unfortunately his tenure was cut by his death the following year at the age of 65.

Another biographical sketch "okayed by Dr. Chapman" is located in the Library of the Museum of Fine Arts. It, too, is not dated but must have been written after 1938 when his monograph, "The Pottery of Santo Domingo Pueblo," was published. We are fortunate because the biography contains the following information:

> With Carlos Vierra, he was appointed to finish a set of six murals on the life of St. Francis of Assisi begun by Donald Beauregard, who died after completing only a section of one. Chapman painted the two side panels of the triptych, "The Renunciation of Santa Clara", the "Apotheosis", and "the Conversion of Saint Francis". The murals were completed and installed in Saint Francis Auditorium of the "New Museum" (now the Fine Arts Musuem) in time for its dedication in 1917.

This information saves us a quandary and a good deal of time. The style of painting of the central panel of the "Santa Clara" triptych is carefully repeated in the "Apotheosis" and adequately in the side panels of the "Santa Clara" triptych. The completed painting of the "Conversion" does not show the same technical use of paint. Either Chapman changed his technique for this panel or it was redone after he had finished it. At any rate Chapman may be given credit for the three murals in question, except for Beauregard's own panel. Carlos Vierra undoubtedly executed the ramaining three paintings. Before a discussion of the panels done by Chapman and Vierra, the latter should be introduced.

Carlos Vierra was a most interesting personality to be associated with the Saint Francis mural project. A very handsome man, gifted with a keen sense of art, he was efficient as a painter, a designer, and architect, photographer, and writer. He was very active socially and married a very charming wife. He was leaven to the cultural ambiance of Santa Fe.

Carlos Vierra came to Santa Fe in 1904 a long way about. Born at Moss Landing near Monterey, California, he was of Portuguese parentage from the Azores. At 22 he went to San Francisco to study art and remained for two years at the end of which time he sailed aboard the "Roanoke" for New York. His father had been a seaman before him but once at his destination Vierra worked as a marine illustrator. Poor health sent him to Santa Fe where the climate was dry and good for his poor respiratory condition. He stayed and eventually, in 1905, bought a photography shop on the Plaza. To further his income he joined the New Mexico National Guard in 1906 and became a crack shot with the rifle. With his shop across the Plaza from the Palace of the Governors it was inevitable that Vierra came to be very friendly with the staff of the School of American Archaeology and of the Museum of New Mexico. He even joined the staff himself in 1912. He supported enthusiastically the attempts of Jesse Nusbaum and Sylvanus Morley to define and promote the Santa Fe style. He wrote essays analysing and praising the type of architecture being developed and designed several wining elevations of houses in that manner for a local competition in 1913. He was one of Hewett's group. When Hewett needed an artist to paint some very large murals of Mayan cities for the San Diego Exposition, Vierra was the man selected. Vierra did four of them in a studio in Tesuque and the other two on the site at San Diego. For two of the panoramas he even accompanied Hewett on an expedition to Honduras and Guatemala in 1914. Hewett was so pleased with his work that he appointed him, along with Chapman, to complete quickly Beauregard's work on the Saint Francis murals. He was responsible for the Columbus panel, the Mayan triptych and for the "Building of the Missions."

Even Frank Springer was attracted to Vierra. In 1918, he bought a parcel of land for the artist to create a Santa Fe house. He paid for construction materials as Vierra built his adobe home. It took three years and still stands as the best model of the domestic use of the Santa Fe style.

Another important relationship developed between Vierra and John Gaw Meem, preeminent architect at Santa Fe for four decades. They collaborated on "Las Acequias," an estate near Nambe built for Chicagoan Cyrus McCormick III, completed in 1930. It is a subtle and beautiful house and again a model for the style in an authentic, romantic way.

In terms of authorship of the paintings of the Saint Francis cycle, there is no question but that Donald Beauregard established the subject matter for each composition and created sufficient of each design to formulate the whole series. The one scene that is completely his is the "Renunciation of Santa Clara" *(Color Section F)*. This has been discussed before so there is no need to do so again except to point out that in addition to the influence of Puvis de Chavannes, Beauregard used color in this instance even more sparingly, with very little contrast of value or intensity, resulting in a calm, flat effect. Color is used, blended with white or black to model the landscape and figures in an unobtrusive way. The figures are isolated from the atmosphere of the open park. In spite of what he said in his letters, Beauregard's figures are delineated in an academic style, self-conscious poses illustrating idealized emotional reactions to events. The side panels of the Santa Clara composition depart somewhat from the style of the central section, although conforming to the preparatory unfinished painting that Beauregard had begun for each. On the left, Beauregard developed a composition recalling the fresco by Benozzo Gozzoli of the "Journey of the Magi" in the chapel of the Medici-Riccardi Chapel in Florence. The throng has been brought up to date somewhat by the blandness and correct self-conscious poses they assume. The scene becomes devoid of excitment, both emotional and pictorial. Chapman, responsible for the two wings of the composition, changed very little, a gesture or a slight shift of posture, but he essentially kept the original concept of Beauregard (Figure 10).

The "Apotheosis," less complete when given to Chapman, has correspondingly been more altered *(Color Section A and Figure 4)*. Philosophy has turned his profile to the foreground. The upper torso of Art has been modestly covered and she holds her attributes instead of her chin. These are minor alterations yet they tone down the interpretation and make less classical the personifications. The painting of the "Conversion of Saint Francis" was changed considerably by Beauregard as shown by an early watercolor sketch *(Color Section G and Figure 11)*. The lateral composition places the young Saint Francis between the Chapel of San Damiano and far off Assisi, between his future avocation and his family tradition. The second sketch, very similar to the mural as completed by Chapman, presents Francis at a slightly later moment at which the Saint has made up his mind and is probably responding to the call of God to get busy on behalf of the Church.

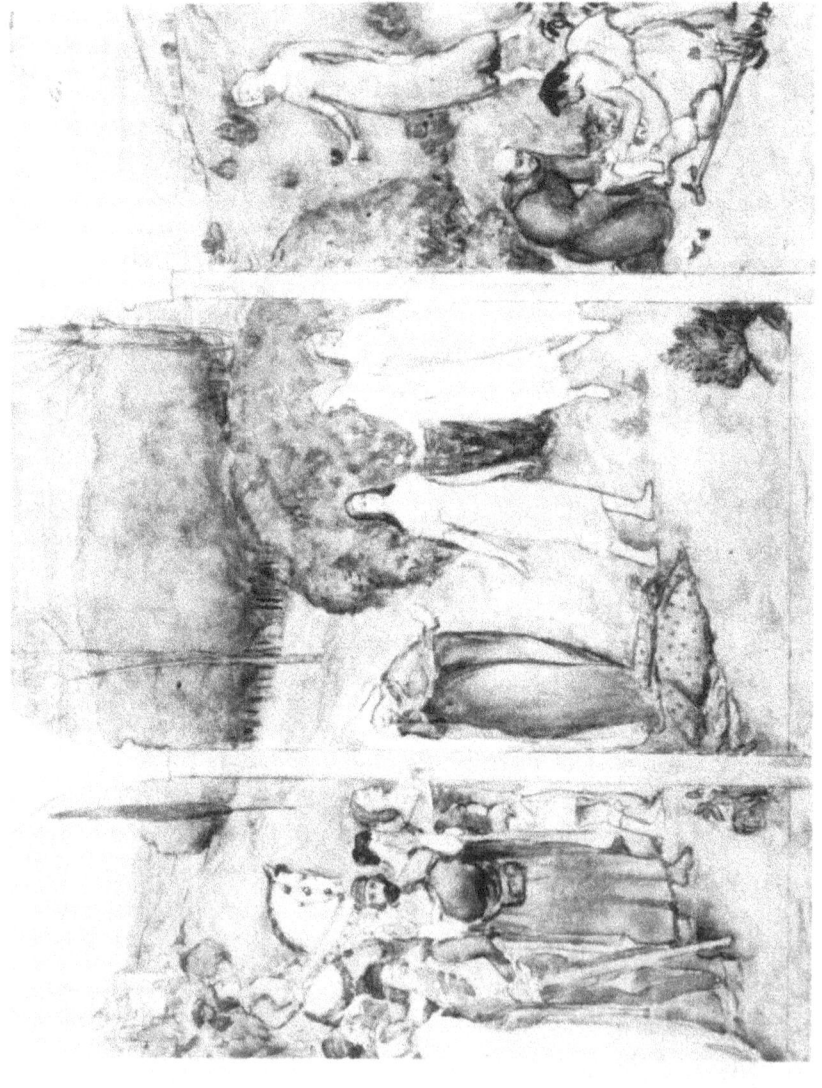

Figure 10:   *"Renunciation of Santa Clara," Donald Beauregard.*

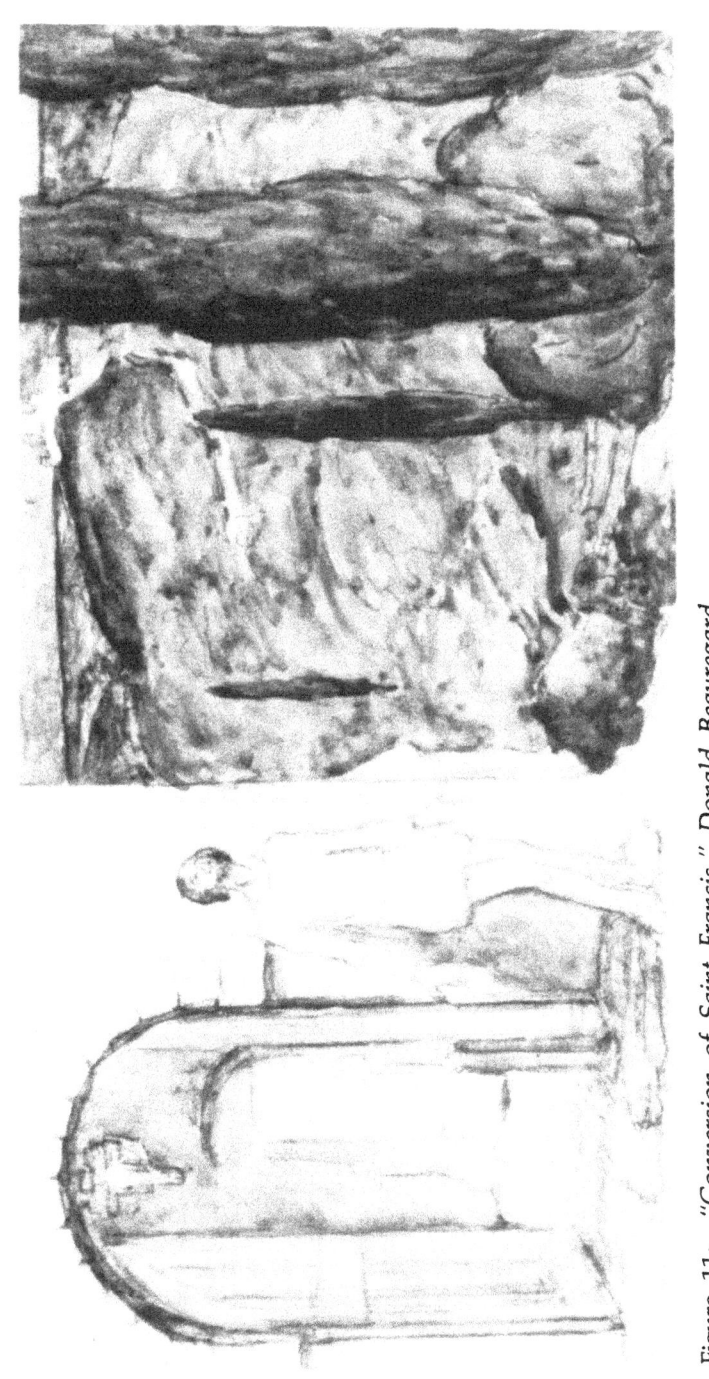

Figure 11: *"Conversion of Saint Francis," Donald Beauregard.*

There are no other oil paintings by Chapman available for comparison. There are several architectural renderings that Chapman did of the new buildings at San Diego and Santa Fe. They are, as expected, clear, thin-lined, and pastel in color, flooded with light. His figure sketches for the murals are correct, attractive academic studies and show sympathy for Beauregard's French style. Apparently he was faithful to the project as he received it and he maintained, although he mitigated somewhat, the content Beauregard had established.

Beauregard, as his letter tells us, did a satisfactory drawing of the Columbus mural *(Figure 12)* and then changed it twice *(Color Section H and B)* by placing the sailing fleet further in the sky from the figures. Otherwise his final sketch accords well with what Carlos Vierra completed. Vierra's painting technique, however, was much freer, broader, and with broken color, reflecting the experiments of the Impressionists. Vierra was not an Impressionist but he was freer with his brush than Chapman and much more colorful. His work has a greater swing of rhythm and exuberance of execution.

Apparently Beauregard did not get so far with the Maya panel as the Columbus one. At any rate, Vierra took more liberties with the sketch in making the final painting *(Color Section C and Figure 13)*. Beauregard isolated the friar by silhouetting his upper body against the sky. The cross he clasps is quite short and held out with strength. The cross becomes the nexus of the whole scene, with opposing forces of Spaniards to the left and Native Americans on the right. The soldier's pikes rise to heaven equalling the height of the Mayan altar to which the Maya are clinging. Directly in front of the Franciscan a native kneels with head bowed as the soldiers advance, their horses

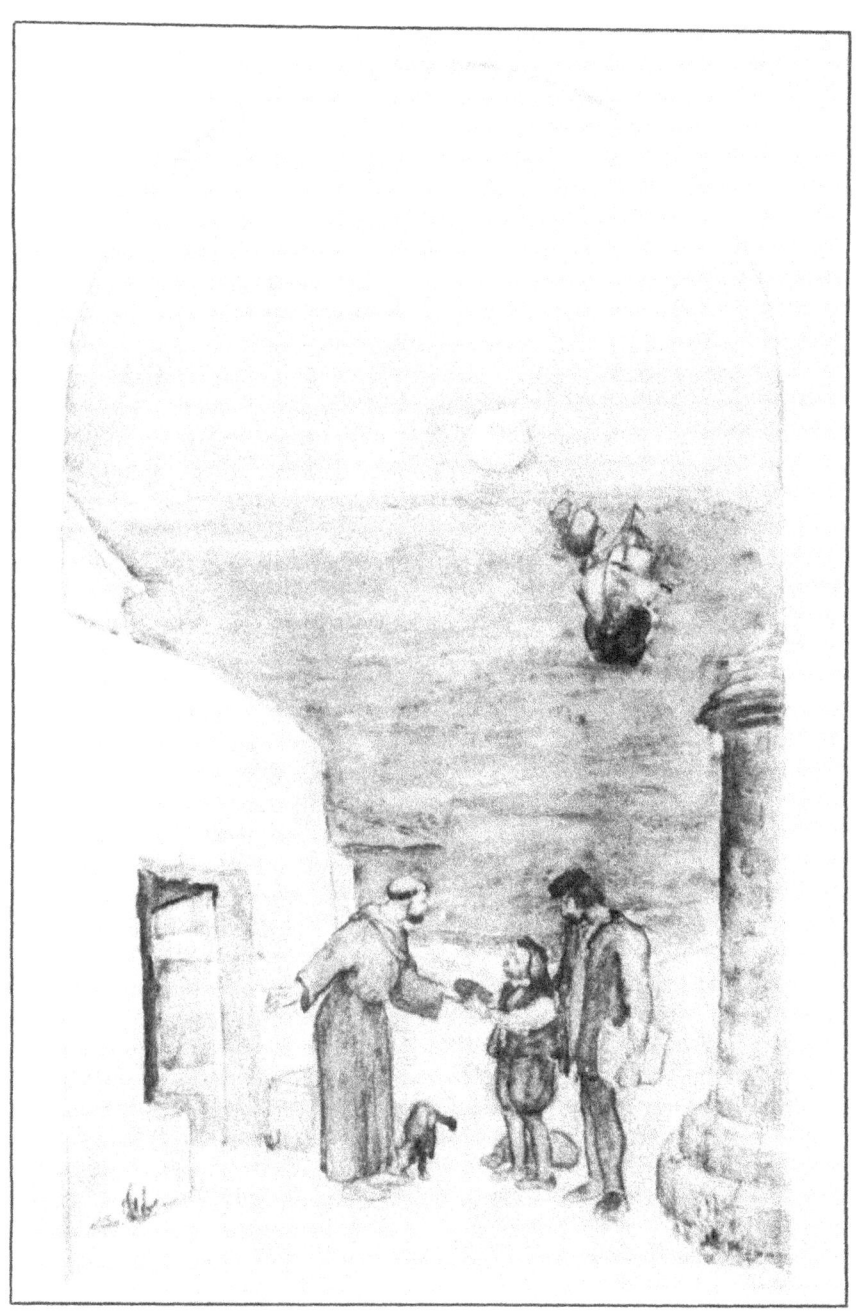

Figure 12:   *"Vision of Columbus at La Rábida,"* Donald Beauregard.

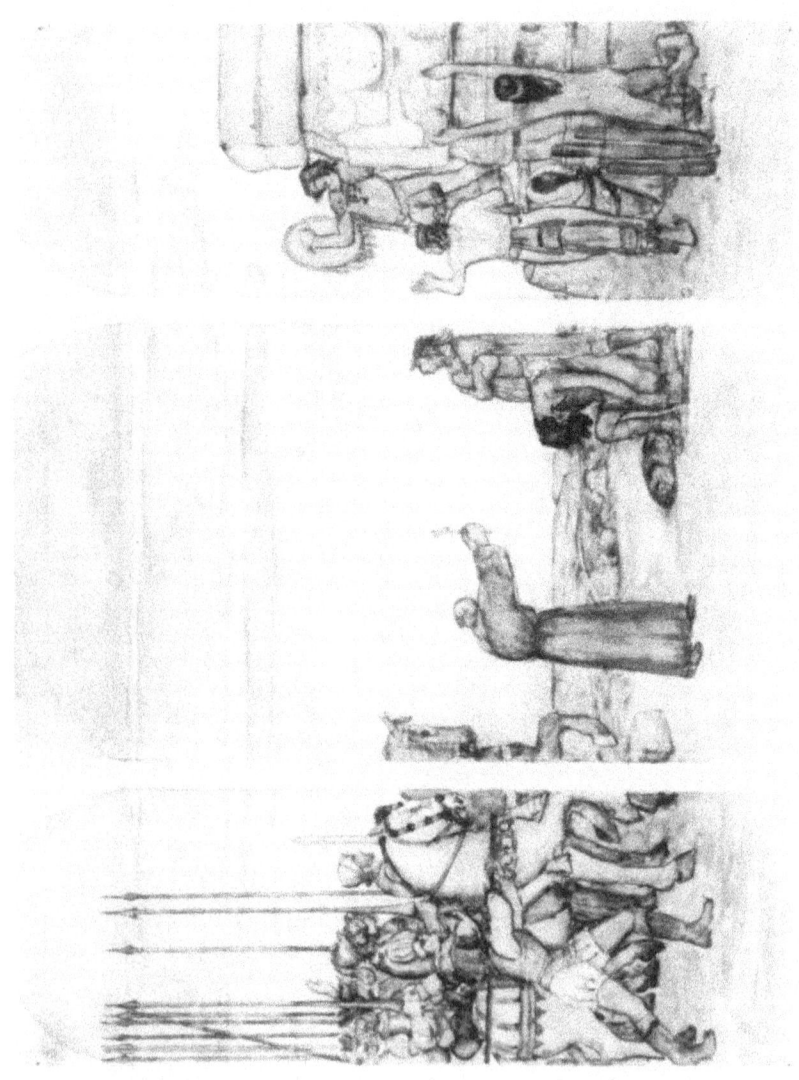

Figure 13:   *"Preaching to the Mayas," Donald Beauregard.*

stepping proudly. A fully armed Spaniard holds his lance on the level pointing beyond the friar, ready for action. Vierra calmed things down and made the scene more magnificent like a pageant. Gone is the forward movement of the Spaniards replaced by a stasis because the lances, flags, horses and men are all vertically poised. The priest, almost in the same position as in the sketch, holds a cross with an elongated base bar. He is now almost hidden against the background and the cross has lost it menace. The Maya are magnificently dressed, and dressed rather accurately in an archeological sense just as the buildings are no longer vaguely Central American but derived from specific structures at Chichen Itza. The scene has lost its religious ferocity and becomes filled with panoply.

The "Building of the Missions" *(Color Section D and Figure 14)* Vierra also adjusted to his own interest. Beauregard's arch was made less important and not so complete. More importantly for the expression of the scene, Vierra took away the hammers used by the monk in the left middle-ground and replaced the one resting in the foreground by a compass. The three monks are also preoccupied by their sketch. Vierra lessened the manual occupation Beauregard suggested and also reduced the bulk of the foreground figures. Overall, he gave a greater uninterrupted view of the Native Americans and the landscape.

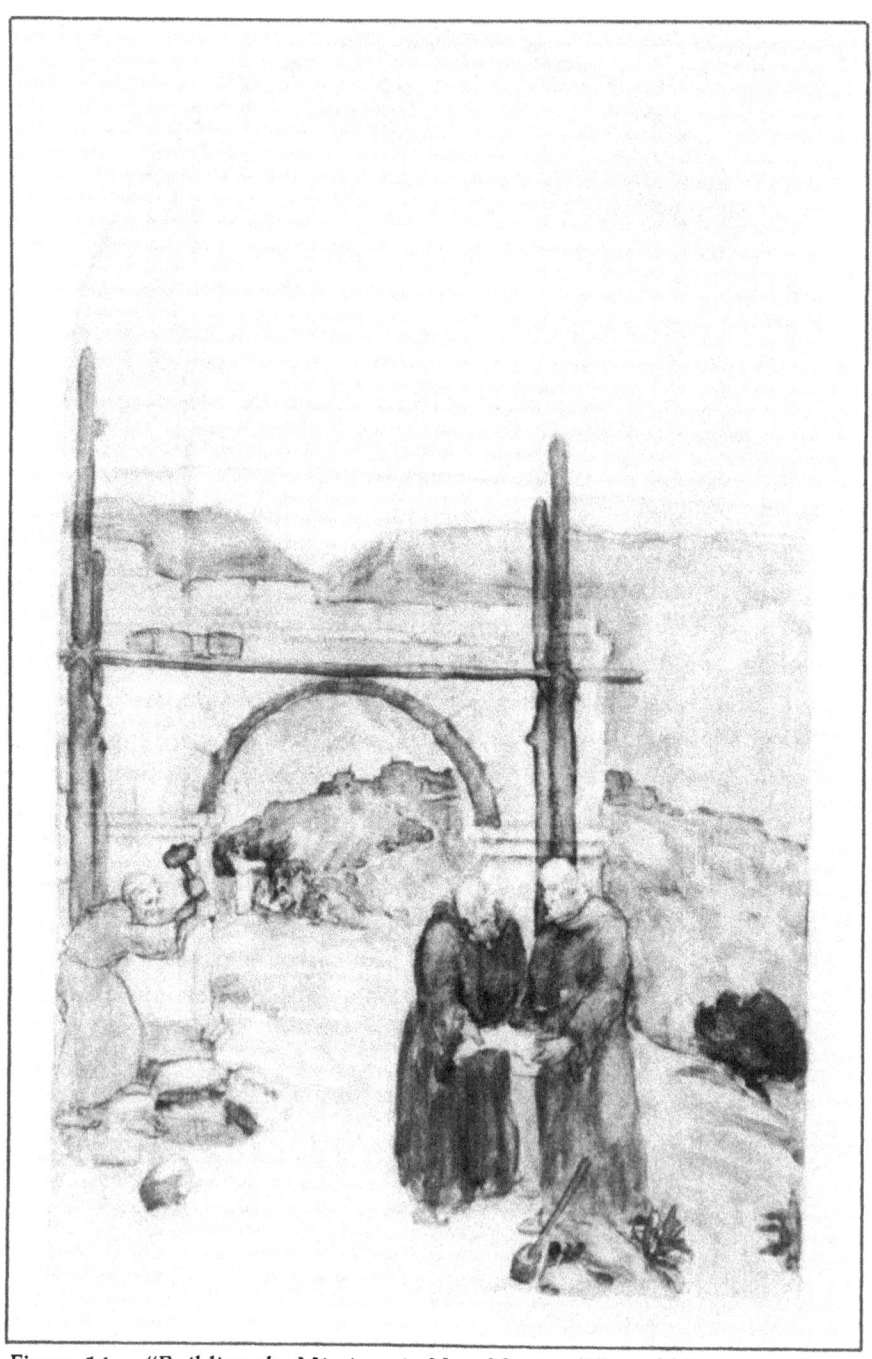

Figure 14: *"Building the Missions in New Mexico,"* Donald Beauregard.

CONCLUSION

The Saint Francis murals of Santa Fe subtly reveal many of the cultural aspirations prevalent in that small New Mexico town just before the United States joined the Allies during the First World War. One could properly expand the locale of Santa Fe and say that a great deal of the citizens of the United States supported similar aspirations as those expressed at the Saint Francis Auditorium. The message of the murals is one of optimism, of place in a paradise for man, of the dominance of the white civilization of Europe, perfected in America. Tolerance, religious plurality, self-confidence for a radiant future, these ideas still speak from the murals, albeit rather softly now.

The murals are unobtrusive in the hall and are experienced as a positive part of the whole without distraction. One can gaze at them passingly without attempt to interpret their scenes or the sense of their sequence and enjoy them as satisfyingly decorative. They were, however, conceived as enhancement for the City of Santa Fe. Prestigious in their very nature, the murals would bring attention to the positive role art played in the community. They would also glorify the name of the city's titular Saint and the New World achievements attributed to the monastic order he founded.

The specific choice of scenes was probably made by Edgar Lee Hewett, Director of the Museum of New Mexico, in consultation with a small circle of enthusiastic friends. Their desire was apparently to link the popular Saint Francis with the discovery of America, the conversion of the natives to Christianity, and the missionary activity in the Rio Grande Valley, even at Santa Fe itself.

Hewett was a very good judge of the quality of a man and, as events proved, selected his subordinates and supporters with great acumen. In this vein, he encouraged the young Donald Beauregard, a Mormon from Utah, to develop his artistic career abroad. Twice the painter went to Europe; the second time supplied by grants through Hewett's intervention. Hewett also suggested a commission in the Southwest for Beauregard when he returned. This was to result in the Saint Francis murals. At first they were ordered for the California-Panama Exhibition at San Diego, for which Hewett was Director of Exhibits. Beauregard conscientiously wrote his benefactor, Frank Springer, about his progress, his expenditures, and his health. The latter prevented his completion of the cycle of the murals commissioned by Hewett. The artist died of cancer. The murals were never sent to San Diego and were eventually installed in the Saint Francis Auditorium, having been completed by Kenneth Chapman and Carlos Vierra.

The pleasantness of the Saint Francis cycle of paintings adds great comfort to the strength of the architecture of the great Auditorium, designed by Isaac Hamilton Rapp, the architect selected by Hewett's circle to formulate their need for an identifiable regional style, based on Hispanic experiences in the past. This Rapp most successfully did, establishing the parameters of the monumental expression of the Santa Fe Style.

BIBLIOGRAPHY

Briggs, Peter."Carlos Vierra: His Role and Influence in the Maya Image." *The Maya Image in the Western World*, Peter Briggs, ed. Albuquerque: University of New Mexico Press, 1986.

Chauvenet, Beatrice. *Hewett and Friends*. Santa Fe: Museum of New Mexico Press, 1983.

Morley, Sylvanus Griswold. *The Ancient Maya*. Palo Alto, California: Stanford University Press, 1946.

Roth, Leland M. *McKim, Mead, and White, Architects*. New York, 983. Sheppard, Carl D. *Creator of the Santa Fe Style, Isaac Hamilton Rapp, Architect*. Albuquerque: University of New Mexico Press, 1988.

Shele, Linda and Mary Ellen Miller. *The Blood of Kings*. Fort Worth, Texas: Kimball Art Museum, 1986.

Tydeman, William E. "Later I Paid People to do Nice Pictures, John Gaw Meem and Architectural Photography." *New Mexico Architect*, Jan./Feb. 1987.

Wattenmaker, Richard. *Puvis de Chavannes and the Modern Tradition*. Toronto: Art Gallery of Ontario, 1975. *El Palacio* 1, no. 1, 1913; 2, vol. 1, 1914.

Museum of New Mexico, Museum of Fine Arts Library, the Beauregard File and the Chapman File.

Museum of New Mexico, Historical Library, Mss. Box 19, File 1, and Box 21, File 2.

INDEX